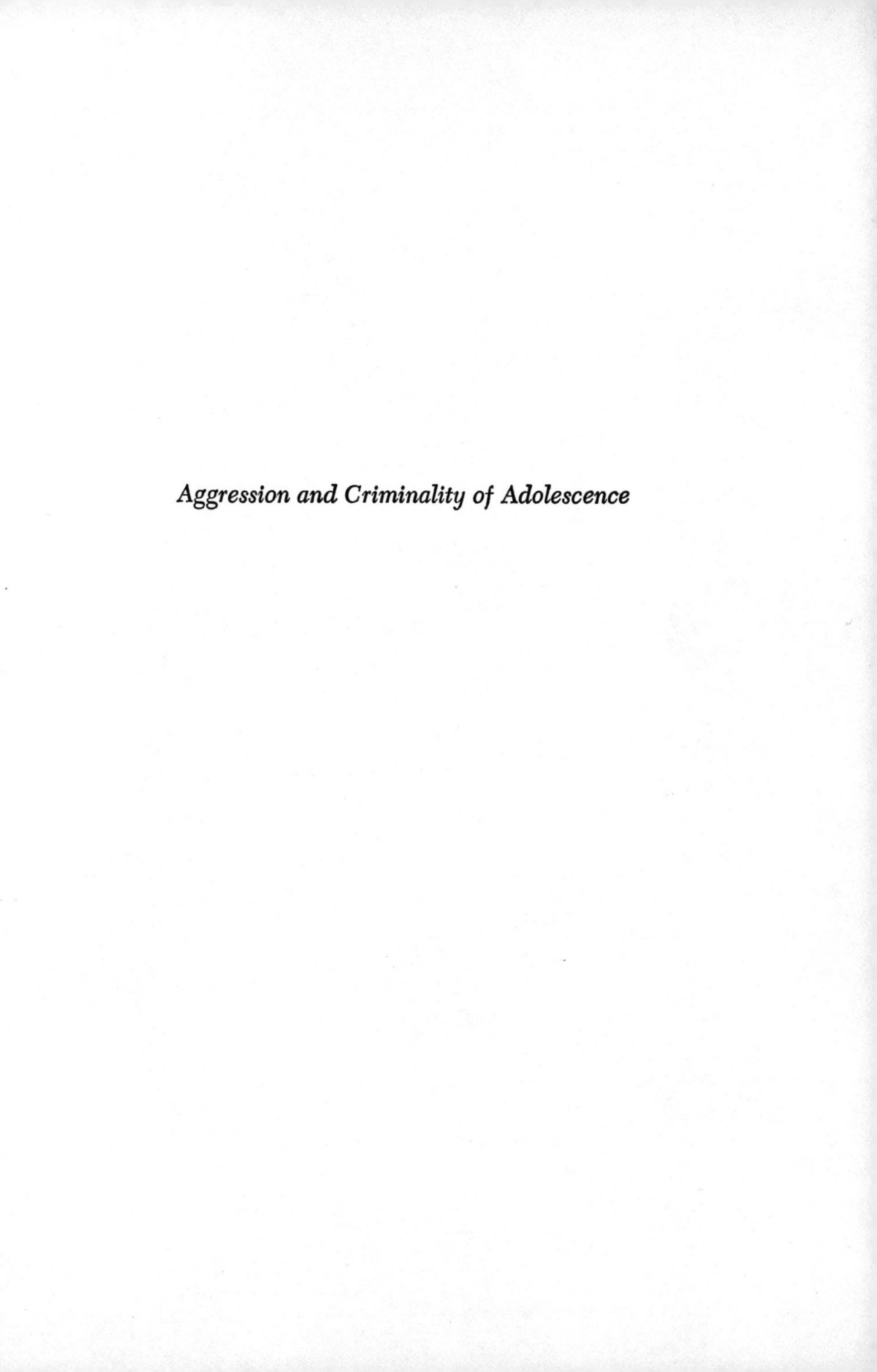

Aggression and Criminality of Adolescence

Aggression
and
Criminality
of Adolescence

Emanuel J. Martinez, Ph.D.

An Exposition-University Book

Exposition Press   **Hicksville, New York**

To my mother, Josephine Napolitano.
Trust, understanding, motivation,
concern, sincerity, love,
and tenderness are all to be found in her;
without her assistance very little
would have been accomplished in my life.
They just do not come any finer.

Contents

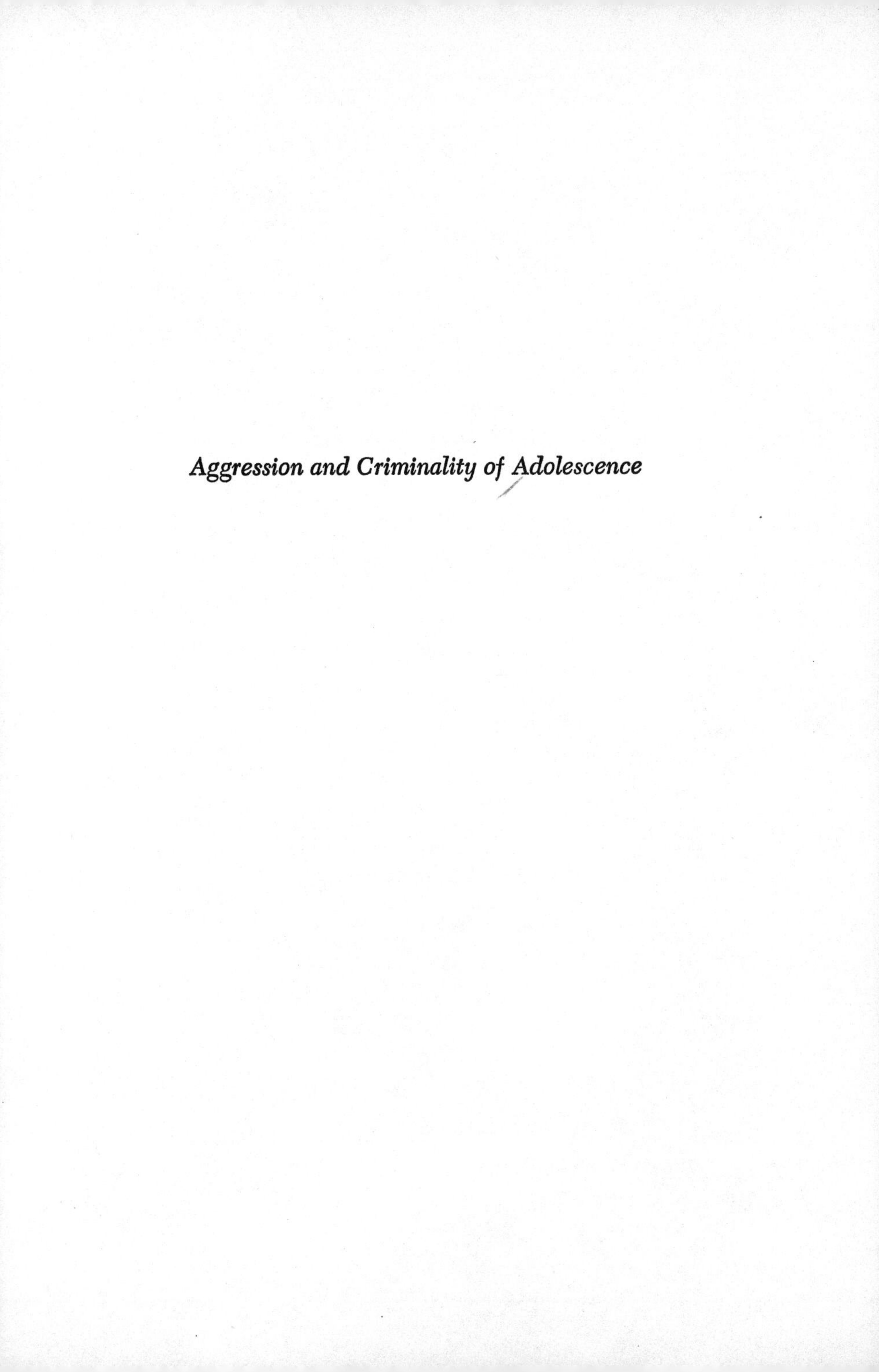

Aggression and Criminality of Adolescence

Introduction

Aggression has been defined and subdivided in many ways.
Some distinguish between "aggression" and "violence," stating
that violence involves physical injury while aggression relates
to psychological harm. Some separate the terms "aggression"
and "aggressive." Recent terminology goes as far as to at times
insinuate that aggression is a positive quality, relating it to
motivation and creative energy. *Webster's Seventh New Collegiate Dictionary* states that it is "an offensive action or procedure; an unprovoked attack; the practice of making attacks
or encroachments." It continues to define "aggressive" as marked
by "combative readiness or obtrusive energy; self-assertive,
unpleasant forwardness or brash self-confidence."

Jeffrey H. Goldstein uses the terms "violence" and "aggression" synonomously, defining them both as "behavior of which
the intent is the physical or psychological injury of another."[1]
He feels that "aggressive behavior used by someone to achieve
a personal goal, such as wealth or power, and which may be
perceived by the actor as justified (or even nonaggressive) is a
primary cause of the aggressive and criminal behavior of
others."[2]

Nevertheless, to date there is no clearly defined scientific
explanation of aggression. Sigmund Freud,[3] and more recently
Anthony Storr,[4] considered it a human instinct. Nikolaas Tinbergen, in an October 28, 1968 article in the *New York Times,*
describes it both instinctively and environmentally.[5] Gordon
Allport suggests that it is a human "capacity."[6]

Fredric Wertham[7] and Ashley Montague[8] state that aggression is predominately a product of environmental factors.
Konrad Lorenz explains the apparent nature of aggression and

the part it plays in the sexual and social everyday lives of animals.[9]

However, even though many scientists readily concede that instinctive and territorial aggressiveness is a life-supporting force among animals, some insist that human beings are somehow motivated quite differently.

James G. Fraser,[10] and more recently J. Bronowski,[11] detailed a number of rituals within ancient cultures. Each discusses how the custom of sacrifice generally related in some way a cleansing of sins by the ritualistic death of a scapegoat—be it animal or human. On some occasions the king himself became the victim through means of his own violent death, symbolizing an inward type of responsibility for the misdeeds of his subjects. Whenever the community might gather to stone its king to death, it was not done so in order to relieve the participants of violence by allowing them to practice it (catharsis), but rather served as a warning against socially unacceptable aggression. Any ritual murder evoked shame, guilt, and sorrow, precipitating throughout the community a collective humility.

It will be the purpose of this thesis to show how aggression and its ramifications are a direct result of the learning processes primarily. In no way will its intention be to infer that chemical, electrical, or any other physiological explanations have no meaning where the understanding of aggression is concerned; but it will attempt to demonstrate how these factors tend to play a secondary role in most cases.

Historically speaking, the answer to the question of whether aggression is innate or learned has changed drastically from one train of thought to another. As a result of the ever-changing and different attitudes toward violence, there remain in both our social and judicial systems techniques and solutions with regard to reduction, control, and elimination of violence, all of which are heirs of inconsistency, not only with one another, but also with current scientific thinking on the issue.

The point to be stressed with regard to the above fact is not that scientific thought changes over time. Obviously, constructive thought patterns change as new information is acquired.

However, the focal point here will be that both formal and informal policies, as well as controls which are used to reduce aggression, are influenced by whether aggression is conceived of as innate or learned.

The innumerous research and overall intense scientific study of animal behavior throughout the middle of the twentieth century leans toward the instinctual pole with regard to aggression. This trend is due a great deal to three major influences: the accounts of aggression materialized by ethologists Konrad Lorenz, Desmond Morris, and Robert Ardrey; the popularity and pervasiveness of Freudian theory; and the persuasive, dramatic research on electrical and chemical stimulation of the brain. In brief, Lorenz, Morris, and Ardrey suggest that there is ample evidence to show that our animal ancestors were instinctively violent beings, and that since we are descendants of them in one form or another, it logically follows that we too must possess basic destructive impulses in our genetic composition. Lorenz states that "there cannot be any doubt, in the opinion of any biologically minded scientist, that intraspecific aggression is, in man, just as much of a spontaneous instinctive drive as it is in most other higher vertebrates."[12]

One aspect of the physiology of aggression that has received a great deal of publicity is the "XYY Syndrome." Here a close relationship is made between aggression and sexual behavior. However, Ashley Montague points out that the XYY phenomenon is not a syndrome that reliably leads to particular behaviors, but an anomaly that, depending upon environmental circumstances, may lead to a wide variety of possible behaviors.

Freud initially proposed that only one instinctive force existed that motivated human behavior—the "life instinct" or Eros. However, his inability to explain the extreme negative qualities surrounding, for example, a world war, led him to modify his theory by adding to it a second force—Thanatos or the "death instinct." Freud felt that societies must learn to "control" the expression of both the life and death instincts. He concluded that the necessary control was felt through the social mores and rules regulating sexual and aggressive conduct.

Present-day psychoanalytic theorists, following for the most part Freud's basic work, maintain the notion that aggression is indeed an instinctive drive. They maintain in conjunction with that idea that aggression must be released periodically in order for it not to reach an intensity of such a level that its expression becomes uncontrollable, spontaneous, or possibly dangerous to an existent society. Norman E. Zinberg and Gordon A. Fellman go as far as to suggest that war itself aids in the discharge of aggression not only for the soldiers fighting the war, but for the civilian onlookers as well.[13] This line of thought suggests that any updated society must eventually accept violence as a part of human nature. It suggests that this supposed essential part of human nature is not essential either because it is good or bad, but simply because it is there. Likewise, Rollo May discusses ways by which aggression may be sublimated.[14] Edward Glover even states that crime is what should be expected from man—a naturally wild animal—when there is any attempt made to domesticate him.[15]

This thesis will demonstrate how the control and possibly the elimination of human aggression may be attained, especially in the younger generation; how a meaningful and comprehensible combination of theory and practice may be materialized to help deal with the difficulties caused by aggressive acts; how the learning (socialization) process is involved with teaching a society's young, impressionable minds both crime and violence, though perhaps unintentionally; and how anthropological theories can all be shown to support the idea that aggression and criminality are primarily the result of the teaching/learning process.

One society that will be studied somewhat will be the Yanomamo Indians of southern Venezuela and northern Brazil, a people who have shown themselves to be an excellent example of a rather unique culture. These Indians are among the most violent, fierce, and competitive groups presently known to anthropologists.

Two other tribes to be discussed will be the Dani Tribe of New Guinea and the Warao Tribe of Venezuela, the former stressing war and painful role playing, the latter encouraging painless and bloodless aggression. Nevertheless, even these societies can have their aggressiveness shown to be a product of situations and circumstancs associated with the environment— for example, the opportunity theory. Also to be discussed will be how learned goals, needs, desires, and wants can all be traced to different forms of aggression, particularly when these goals and needs are not or can not be obtained.

| Throughout most of the research on aggression there have been three bases that have led scholars to categorize aggression (aggressive acts) into three subtypes: (a) theoretical, (b) empirical, and (c) legal./ The latter simply makes distinctions between American and English law and their relationship to legal (socially acceptable) and illegal (socially unacceptable) violence. The empirical categorization stems from the fact that different acts of aggression have, or at least seem to have, different antecedent conditions or different amounts of force, premeditation, or emotional arousal involved. Thus such distinctions are made by social psychologists between angry aggression, emotional excitement immediately prior to aggressive acts, and non-angry aggression; between direct aggression, which is aggression shown toward the frustrator, and displaced aggression, which is aggression placed onto a target other than the frustrator (frustration-aggression theory, 1939, Dollard, Doob, Miller, Mowrer, and Sears). Lastly, the category "theoretical" is based on the fact that different theories are capable of explaining and predicting limited instances of aggression, which necessitates dividing aggression into categories according to ease of explanation. Each of these categories—i.e., theoretical, empirical, and legal—will be interwoven throughout this thesis to aid in formulating the proposed overview of theory and research on human aggression, which can serve as a foundation for the control and future elimination of not only violent crimes, but also of violence itself; an overview that can discuss the many social problems that are assimilated with violence, and that would also be reduced, if not completely liquidated, should violence be better understood and thus dealt with at its own level.

Again, there is no scientific description of aggression or violence that will permit anyone to infer an operative set of standards which is "good" or "bad," acceptable or unacceptable, circumscribing aggression in human affairs. Humans, though, have been violent since their cave days. Future research will have to demonstrate to us a better understanding of the psychological, physiological, and biological causes of aggression. However, for the present, what is needed is an operational system of theories coupled with and resulting from scientific endeavor, which will enable everyone concerned to formulate rules regarding conduct whereby society and its functions can cumulatively materialize without an overall threat to human existence or human development in general.

Etiology

To discuss the causes and origin of human aggression is somewhat difficult, basically because the terms used to represent aggression convey so many different and controversial senses or meanings. To begin with, there is no distinct line dividing those forms of aggression that are almost deplorable within a particular social context, and those that must be maintained if human survival and growth are to prevail. When a youngster, for example, rebels against authority, he is by all means acting aggressively, but he is also manifesting a drive toward independence, which is necessary and valuable to the process of growth. To strive for unlimited power can produce disastrous results, but the drive to solve conflicts, or to fight for survival, underlies the greatest of human achievements.

Some scholars define aggression as a response which follows frustration, or as an act which has its main intent directed toward the injury of an organism or an organism surrogate. These definitions, however, impose limits upon the concept of aggression which are not in accord with the underlying facts of what has been sometimes referred to as "human nature." It is worth noticing, for instance, that many words and expressions used to describe innumerous situations are aggressive in nature, even when aggression is not necessarily intended, or perhaps intended but unconsciously so. Problems are "attacked." We get our "teeth into things." We "fight for what is right." A field of endeavor is "mastered." We "knock them dead." Difficulties are "struggled with" and "eventually conquered."

Aggression is not only a necessary safeguard against possible attack, but it is also the basis of motivation, of the attainment of independence, and of defining one's identity. Paradoxically, though, the very qualities that have led to man's extraordinary accomplishments are also those that are most capable of destroying him.

The present concern of Western society with the problem of aggression is catalyzed by the reality of an ever-increasing crime rate, and more traumatically by the fear of total annihilation via nuclear warfare.

When Sigmund Freud commenced his research into the human mind toward the close of the nineteenth century, he had little to say regarding aggression. At this time when the mental climate in Vienna was one in which sex was socially secretive, it was natural that Freud should have allotted so little importance to aggression compared to sexuality.

Alfred Adler believed that "striving for superiority" was the dominant motive behind human behavior. Adler's concept became increasingly and progressively modified with time. According to Ernest Jones, it was during the year of 1908 that Adler suggested that there might be a primary aggressive instinct, which eventually was expressed as a "will to power," which was superseded by the term "striving for superiority."[16] It was not until 1915 that Freud first wrote of aggression as primary and distinct from sexuality. By 1920 this new concept had materialized into a theory of the "death instinct." Even when Freud came to recognize that there was something like an aggressive instinct in man, he concluded that it was primarily self-destructive rather than directed toward mastering the external world.

Freud's final view came to be that there were simply two groups of instincts; namely, "erotic instincts which are always trying to collect living substances together into even larger unities, and the death instincts, which act against that tendency and try to bring living matter back into an inorganic condition. The cooperation and opposition of these two forces produce the phenomena of life to which death puts an end."[17] Also, "In the psycho-analytical theory of the mind we take it for granted that the course of mental processes is automatically regulated by the pleasure principle: that is to say, we believe that any given process originates in an unpleasant state of tension and thereupon determines for itself such a path that its ultimate issue coincides with the relaxation of this tension, i.e., with avoidance of pain or with production of pleasure."[18]

|And so, in Freud's view, aggression against the external world was ultimately the result of the death instinct being blocked by erotic and self-preservative instincts. |Although the death instinct must finally conquer, since everyone dies, it was thought that, so long as life persisted, its natural expression was inhibited:

> Although the acceptance of a death instinct is in one sense an admission of a primary aggressive drive, the concept yet implies that aggression directed against the external world is a secondary phenomenon which would not exist unless the primary instinct was somehow interfered with. Thus, although those who hopefully believe that man's aggression is invariably the result of frustration have not necessarily accepted the existence of a death instinct, yet there is nothing even in Freud's later work which would support the idea of a positive, primary aggressive drive; and hence nothing which is obviously opposed to the idea that some kind of frustration is always antecedent to aggression.[19]

According to Anthony Storr,

> . . . in man, as in other animals, there exists a physiological mechanism which, when stimulated, gives rise both to subjective feelings of anger and also to physical changes which prepare the body for fighting. This mechanism is easily set off, and, like other emotional responses, it is stereotyped and, in this sense, "instinctive." Just as one angry cat is very like another angry cat, so one angry man or woman closely resembles another at the level of physiological responses; although, of course, the way in which human beings adapt to and control their feelings of rage differs widely according to training.[20]

W. B. Cannon showed that bodily changes in pain, hunger, fear, and rage serve the function of "efficiency in physical struggle."[21] He believed that the arousal of emotion served the biological purpose of preparing an animal to take action, regardless whether the response was stimulated by fear (possible flight) or by rage (possible attack).

From innumerous experiments on animals, some have suggested that there is a small area at the base of the brain in which the feelings of anger originate—namely, the hypothalamus. When an animal's hypothalamus is stimulated artificially by electricity, the animal will show all the signs of rage. However, this result does not *necessarily* mean that there is anything in the environment which would in essence and of itself produce aggressive behavior, as, for example, electrical stimulation does.

That there exists a physiological mechanism that is in some way related to aggression, at least in some instances, is not what is really in question. Self-preservation and individual growth as a necessary reaction to an ever-changing environment demands that any animal possess the "potential" for aggressive behavior. That aggressiveness can be triggered is also not the main issue. Although there is much controversy as to whether aggression is instinctive or not, the question remaining, even when that issue is appeased, is, "Need the trigger be pulled?"

A major part of the disagreement on the issue of aggression, then, is whether or not there is any pressing, internal need for the mechanism to be brought into use; or whether, if the organism were never threatened, aggressive behavior would ever be manifested. This issue becomes paramount with regard to any effective goals which might purport to better control and direct undesirable aggression. It also follows, then, that it is important to determine whether there is in animals and/or humans an internal accumulation of aggressive tension that needs periodic discharge, or whether the aggressive discharge is simply a response to external stimuli, only a "potential" that need never become activated. If the former is the case, what is needed perhaps to control aggression is "outlets for aggression"; if the latter is true, what is required is the avoidance of any stimuli which might excite an undesirable aggressive response.

One difficulty still exists, though, if we speak in terms of "outlets of aggression;" namely, that some studies seem to suggest that the expression alone of aggression does not in and by itself necessarily cause aggression and its forces to be lessened, but rather causes them to be reinforced and perhaps increased. For example, several football coaches have admitted that many extremely aggressive team members became increasingly aggressive as the season progressed, rather than decreasingly so from a supposed burn-out effect. It is a known fact that sports in America are becoming more and more violent, and the more violent they become, the more popular they become. Margaret Meade herself stated, "Put something peaceful on, and the people turn off the set."[22]

Dr. Saul Kapel refutes the idea that catharsis is a desirable way for children to handle aggression, i.e., by means of participating in aggressive games or by watching films or television, which both have a tendency to exploit and dramatize violence.[23]

According to Dr. Kapel, a recent survey by the National Institute of Education stated that there is no evidence to back up theories of catharsis. The report, Dr. Kapel says, states that "while an aggressive kick against a tree may be satisfying to an angry child, the very satisfaction gained by kicking serves as a reward for aggressive behavior, which is likely to be directed toward an individual in the near future."[24]

> Football is a sport and should not be regarded as therapy for frustration. Certainly, a youth who blocks and tackles with great ferocity may temporarily lose some of his frustration and hostility simply because he is tired.
>
> Unfortunately, the aggressiveness he has demonstrated will be applauded by the specators and encouraged by his coach. So his aggressiveness has been rewarded, and if he is young and impressionable, the boy may carry over the "approved" behavior into relationships with individuals off the field.[25]

"Studies indicate," continues Dr. Kapel, "that youngsters who watch violence perpetrated on a TV screen tend to become more, not less, aggressive.[26]

> Aggression begets aggression. We should have clearly learned that fact long ago by observing how one war follows upon

another. And this is as true among individuals as it is for those groups who call themselves nations.

Instead of encouraging a child to act out his hostilities, parents should listen to the angry youngster and, by talking, try to find out what are the seed causes of the anger. Is it just a temporary thing due to a single incident, or is there some relationship or condition that constantly frustrates the youngster so he builds up a constant reservoir of aggressive feelings?

A child must develop the capacity to experience anger and then contain it. You can help the youngster eliminate the reflexive desire to simply lash out and learn that violence does not solve the problem but may lead only to the injury of himself or others.

With this kind of verbal assistance, youngsters can learn to tolerate their anger, enabling them to gradually reestablish their equilibrium and sense of inner harmony.[27]

However, psychologists Seymour and Norma Feshback see aggression as having its roots in the family circle, and show why TV and Hollywood violence may not be as dangerous as we think.[28]

Comparing male and female violence, the Feshbacks feel that although there is considerable evidence to show that boys are more physically aggressive than girls, such evidence is much less consistent when other forms of aggression are examined. Their studies suggest that girls make greater use of indirect forms of aggression than do boys, and that in some circumstances girls can be meaner and more hostile than boys.[29] They suggest that violence crosses class, region, religion, sex, and ethnical boundaries, and is inherent in most animal species. According to Seymour and Norma Feshback, the answer to the question of why boys are more likely to engage in physical violence while girls are more likely to use indirect forms of aggressive behavior rests upon the answer to a more fundamental question —that of where aggression originates.

"Aggressive behavior . . . clearly has roots in our biological make-up and inheritance. Aggression also is a social act and a method of problem solving. Consequently, it is subject to the influence of culture and personality."[30]

Although Freud's biologically oriented views of aggression

imply that it is unlikely that human beings can ever eliminate violence through social change or in the changing of child-rearing practices (which then implies that the most a society can do is to provide socially acceptable outlets for aggressive instincts), some modern-day authors are convinced that there is no essential need for aggressive behavior ever to be manifested. J. P. Scott, for example, says:

> The important fact is that the chain of causation in every case eventually traces back to the outside. There is no physical evidence of any spontaneous stimulation for fighting arising within the body. This means that there is no need for fighting, either aggressive or defensive, apart of what happens in the external environment. . . . This is quite a different situation from the physiology of eating, where the internal processes of metabolism lead to definite physiological changes which eventually produce hunger and stimulation to eat, without any changes in the environment.
>
> We can also conclude that there is no such thing as a simple "instinct for fighting," in the sense of an internal driving force which has to be satisfied. There is, however, an internal physiological mechanism which has only to be stimulated to produce fighting. This distinction may not be important in many practical situations, but it leads to a hopeful conclusion regarding the control of aggression. The internal physiological mechanism is dangerous, but it can be kept under control by external means.[31]

Konrad Lorenz and Nikolaas Tinbergen believe that aggressive behavior is an innate reaction to particular stimulus patterns that the organism encounters within its surroundings—not an instinct simply and necessarily in search of an outlet. Researchers have demonstrated how these stimulus patterns, called releasers, can trigger reactions in animals. For example, whenever a male robin prepares to stake out his territory, he will virtually attack another robin. David Lack has shown that the robin's red breast is the releaser in so far as the defensive robin will threaten a cluster of red feathers and yet totally ignore a brown-breasted live bird.[32]

If one follows the insinuations made by such studies as the one just cited above, he could easily conclude that anyone investigating aggressive behavior in children should also expect to encounter critical events and stimuli—e.g., sudden movements or threatening gestures—that might act as releasers. However, to date, there is very little known about these supposed innate releasers in humans. What is known, though, is that releasers do not work in a simple, automatic manner, even among animals. The triggering effect seems to depend on the animal's past experiences, and upon the physiological state of the animal—e.g., whether the animal is hungry, in pain, in its mating season, or nursing its young.

During the past several years, biologists have focused on biochemical factors which affect an organism's readiness to respond aggressively. Although some of their work suggests that hormone differences between the sexes may be related to sex dissimilarities in aggressive behavior—e.g., the greater physical size and strength of males may contribute to their affinity for violence—yet the single biological differences by and of themselves do not seem to account for, as an example, the great variety of aggressive responses which have been observed in children and adults.

Learning by experience and through cultural expectations is, to this writer, the major cause of sex differences in the way children express or inhibit their aggression. Despite the fact that Freud proposed an instinctive-drive theory, he did not deny the fact that early life experiences might very well initiate some types and expressions of aggressive behavior. He maintained that a frustrating confrontation, intense situation, or painful experience—be it physical or psychological—could eventually project itself into an aggressive reaction, which might manifest itself further into destructive acts or hostile fantasies. It was John Dollard et al., who, after expanding and developing this aspect of Freud's theories, materialized the foundation of the frustration-aggression hypothesis, which basically states that frustration is the primary source of aggressive behavior.

Certainly any growth and maturation process will entail a certain amount and form of frustration. Nevertheless, there are not many present-day behavioral scientists who agree on the validity of the frustration-aggression assumption. What is stressed by innumerous psychologists is that children respond to frustrating situations in a great number of ways. Some youngsters, for example, wait patiently for a thing or event they very much desire, while others become annoyingly anxious over circumstances or material goods, which of themselves are menial, and oftentimes not even actually wanted, needed, or desired by the youngster. Some children will share their most prized toys and other belongings even when they have been abused by other children repeatedly, while others will resent or refuse any form of a sharing process in any situation./

Since there is no reason to believe that what is taught and experienced in childhood—if not retaught or experienced somewhat differently at a later date—will not extend itself into adolescence and adulthood, it follows that there may be similarities between those things which make a child violent, and those things which make anyone violent. Some adolescents, as do some adults, quit after defeat; others, after defeat, become more motivated:

> These individual differences in response to frustration may be due in part to differences in temperament, but they result primarily from differences in learning. Various studies have shown that training can influence and modify a child's response to frustration. A child learns to respond a certain way to being hit accidentally by another child, he learns a different response to being hit deliberately. We teach a child to feel one way if he attains a poor grade because he hasn't studied, and another way if he has been unjustly or arbitrarily graded.[33]

Obviously, society, the family, and peer groups stimulate and reinforce an individual's or, more specifically, a child's behavior and behavior patterns. A youngster who gets attention by smashing something or by hitting another youngster certainly will be more likely to use the same tactics in similar situations in the future. On the other hand, the child who does not receive attention for such behavior may learn alternative approaches, such as ingratiation or cooperation, to achieve the same or even similar goals of attention or possession.

Innumerous studies and follow-ups to those studies clearly

indicate that children who are beaten tend to become parents who beat.[34] Also, most men who beat women come from backgrounds where violence was a common occurrence.[35]

The process of selective reinforcement is one way in which children acquire aggressive and nonaggressive behaviors. Imitation, a more subtle process, also contributes to a child's aggressive behavior patterns. Children oftentimes have demonstrated that they will identify themselves with, and use as models, those whom they love, admire, or even fear. The child copies, simulates, and even admires at times modes of behavior, particularly those of its parents, that have perhaps been, at least overtly or in appearance, discouraged. In other words, children may well at times imitate what they see rather than behave as they are told they should. Parents who beat their children for being violent often do not realize that they are teaching the child, by hitting him or her, that violence is necessary in order to get others to do what you want them to.

Much confusion and ambivalence exists in the American society today. Children, who are well known to be extremely malleable in many instances, are at a disadvantage if they attempt to follow society's rules and regulations. They are told, "Silence is golden," but also, "Speak or forever hold your peace," "Look before you leap," and "He who hesitates is lost." They are faced with the idea, "My one and only love," but also, "Love is more beautiful the second time around."

Society also burdens its youth with strenuous distinctions between the male and the female, most of which are nonsensical. Cigars given to relatives and friends soon after a baby's birth hold blue wrappers for boys and pink wrappers for girls, reading respectively, "It's a boy," "It's a girl," rather than "It's healthy."

Man enjoys believing that he is an animal who acts rationally. However, according to cognitive dissonance theorists, it is more true that man is a rationalizing animal, an animal constantly attempting to appear reasonable to himself and others rather than actually demonstrating such.

Camus went as far as to say that "man is a creature who

spends his entire life in an attempt to convince himself that he is not absurd."[36]

\ Obviously, a child learns much of his aggressive behavior from parents, friends, and other adults, but again, what each child is encouraged to learn may well depend on the child's gender. Culture is not coeducational; there are separate curricula for boys and girls. From early infancy boys and girls receive different treatment from their parents and from society. For example, we encourage vigorous physical activity by boys, and more "feminine" behavior in girls. A boy refusing to fight may quickly be labeled a "fagot," "sissy," or "chicken" by his peers; a girl who engages in physical aggression goes beyond her boundaries as a "lady." \

The foregoing paragraph does not suggest that differences in physique, physical strength, and other biological factors do not contribute to sex differences in aggressive behavior; it is rather suggested that learning is of paramount importance in the determination of a child's behavior.

One way to conceive of the ongoing flow of behavior is to think of it as representing a succession of choices in a series of decision situations. A choice is the behavior of a person who, when faced with a number of possible alternatives of action, acts so as to carry out one of those alternatives in particular.

In the study of learning, psychologists commonly observe choice behavior. Similarly, the study of preferences amounts to the study of choice behavior. Further, psychological scaling proceeds on the basis of observation of choices by a subject in his attempt to discriminate or detect stimuli. And, of course, choices are observed in the widely used multiple-choice technique for assessing a person's knowledge, attitudes, and values. One might argue then that the data of psychology consists importantly of choices made by subjects at stated decision points.

In view of the pervasiveness of choice behavior, it is surprising that, until recently, comparatively little attention has been given by psychologists to the foundations of the act of choice itself. Although choices are observed in studies of learning, motivation, perception, and other psychological fields of speculation, relatively little work has been concerned with choice per se. Since choice is of such significance for anyone interested in the study of human behavior, choice behavior itself may merit intensive formal analysis, namely, theoretical and experimental work directed toward the understanding and explanation of the act of choice.

One approach to the study of such a significant and pervasive phenomenon as choice might be to survey a diversity of choice situations and a variety of choice behaviors in an attempt to identify in these the common features or underlying commonalities.

The alternative path is to identify a single, definite choice situation and to study it in detail. This perspective, as would also the first, considers five major aims: (1) to identify the factors relative to choice behavior in the situation, (2) to propose the relations among these factors, (3) to propose the relations of these factors to choice behavior, (4) to devise a formal mathematical expression of these relations, and (5) to test the adequacy of predictions made from this mathematical model.[37]

It is not the purpose of this paper to get involved with the actual mathematical or fine laboratory research techniques that circumscribe certain professional theories relating to choice and learning—and what each implies with reference to human behavior. Suffice it to say that many studies have been conducted concerning choice behavior in innumerous situations of this sort, and it is commonly observed in these studies that subjects tend to stabilize at predicting two separate events in about the proportions in which they occur.

Any theory of rationality that does not incorporate the concept of utility or subjective value of outcomes is vulnerable to difficulties in the interpretation of behavior.[38] This fact has been recognized at least since the work of Bernoulli (1738).

The term "utility" might be used interchangeably, for this paper's purposes, with the term "subjective value." The utility of an outcome is the value of that outcome to any particular individual. One may speak then of "the utility of a correct response," alluding to some index of the subjective value which a particular individual attaches to responding correctly.

The overall utility of any possible outcome may depend on the subjective value of each of several conceptually distinct aspects of that outcome. To predict choice behavior one must identify the various aspects of the situation to which positive or negative utility is associated.

The concept of dissonance is similar to the concepts of incongruity and imbalance. However, these last two are more like each other than either is like dissonance. In comparing dissonance with the other two conceptions of inconsistency, it is sometimes considered helpful to use the terms "balance" and "imbalance" as generic forms, inclusive also of congruity and incongruity.

A state of cognitive dissonance is said to be a realm of psychological discomfort or tension that motivates efforts to achieve consonance. Dissonance is the name used for a disequilibrium, and consonance, the name for equilibrium.

The notable influence of the theory of cognitive dissonance cannot be explained by the fact that it is a formulation of the inconsistency principle; imbalance and incongruity are more precise formulations. Dissonance theory is influential because it has emphasized a very interesting type of inconsistency, some peculiar aspects of the magnitude of inconsistency and some contemplative ways of inconsistency reduction.

Dissonance theorists have been imaginative in producing ways through which one might reduce conflict. Consider the adolescent, for example, who considers both of these positions to be true: Smoking cigarettes is dangerous to my health; I smoke cigarettes. He might reduce dissonance by giving up smoking and so relinquish belief in the second of the two propositions, or he might somehow decide that smoking someway is not really all that dangerous since the evidence is based strictly on experimental jargon. Leon Festinger, however, suggests that he might control his flow of information, seeking out reports of reassuring research and avoiding the lung cancer statistics. He might also seek out other smokers who would give him support.

When one speaks of "cognitive consequences of compliance," he is referring primarily to an experiment enacted by Festinger and Carlsmith (1959). This study had all subjects spend an hour at some very tedious tasks. When the experimental tasks had been completed, all subjects were told a cover story purporting to explain the purpose of the experiment. The story was largely untrue; it went something like this:

> You have participated in an experiment on the effects of expectation or "set." Some subjects, like yourselves, are enacting the experimental tasks without being given any particular expectation concerning the task. Other subjects, before they start the tasks, encounter someone who has supposedly just finished with the tasks, and they are told that the procedure is "very enjoyable." The person who tells them this is a paid confederate of ours. We are concerned in this experiment with the effect on performance of the anticipation that the tasks will be enjoyable.

All subjects were exposed to this cover story, all subjects had worked at the dull tasks, and, in fact, all subjects had worked without having been given an expectation that the task would be fun.

The outcome of the Festinger and Carlsmith experiment is not an obvious one. One might have expected that the subjects who were strongly rewarded would project an inclination to the favorable rating. However, not the least interesting aspect of the study concerning the results is the fact that the outcomes contradict a reward or punishment principle.

The core notion then of dissonance theory is rather simple: Dissonance is a negative drive state that occurs whenever an individual simultaneously holds two cognitions that are psychologically inconsistent. What some individuals do in order to reduce their inner confusion when this inconsistency exists is somewhat interesting. A few experiments on the subject might help.

Aronson and Carlsmith (1963) predicted that if threats are used to prevent people from performing a desired activity, the smaller the threat, the greater will be the tendency for people

to derogate the activity. They discovered that children who
were threatened with mild punishment for playing with a desired
toy decreased their liking for the toy to a greater extent than
did children who were severely threatened.

Aronson and Mills (1959) reasoned that if people undergo
a great deal of trouble in order to gain admission to a group
that turns out to be a dull and uninteresting one, they will
experience dissonance. The realization that they worked hard
in order to become members of the group is dissonant with
cognitions concerning the negative aspects of the group. One
is not supposed to work hard for nothing. To reduce dissonance,
then, they will eventually distort their actual perception of the
group in a positive direction.

One of the earliest experiments testing derivations from
dissonance theory was performed by Brehm (1956). Brehm
offered individuals a choice between two appliances which they
had previously evaluated. He discovered that in the ensuing
decision, when the subjects reevaluated the alternatives, they
enhanced their liking for the chosen appliance, while simul-
taneously downgrading their evaluation of the appliance not
chosen. The derivation is rather clear then. After making a difficult choice, people experience dissonance; cognitions concerning
any negative attributes of the preferred object are dissonant
with having chosen it; cognitions about positive attributes of
the unchosen object are dissonant with not having chosen it. To
reduce dissonance, then, people tend to emphasize the positive
aspects and deemphasize the negative aspects of the chosen
object; conversely, they emphasize the negative aspects and
deemphasize the positive aspects of the object not chosen.

When discussing the difficulties in the making of precise
predictions from dissonance theory in some situations, it is not
always an easy task to discuss the problem of individual differences. The fact that all people are not the same presents
intriguing problems for dissonance theorists. Basically, though,
there are three ways in which people differ from one another,
which are of major concern to those investigating dissonance
theory: First, people differ in their ability to tolerate dissonance.

It seems reasonable to assume that some people are simply better than others at dissipating the discomfort that dissonance brings. Second, people probably differ in their preferred mode of dissonance reduction. Third, what is dissonant for one person may be consonant for another.[39]

As Aronson pointed out in 1960, many studies have made predictions based upon the tacit assumption that people generally have a high self-concept. Why do many people, particularly adolescents, who have bought new clothes selectively expose themselves to ads about their own chosen styles? Aronson feels that this tendency occurs because of the knowledge that "junky" clothes are dissonant with a high self-concept. But suppose a person had a low self-concept. Then the cognition that he had bought ugly clothes would not be dissonant. If the theory holds any water whatsoever, such a person should engage in innumerous kinds of strange behavior—i.e., exposing himself to ads about other styles of clothing, seeing flaws in the fabric that are not even there, etc. Briefly, then, if a person pictures himself to be an ass, he will expect himself to behave like an ass; consequently, wise and reasonable behavior on his part should actually arouse dissonance. One of the advantages of this kind of outlook is that it allows one to separate the effects of dissonance from other hedonic effects; that is, people with high self-concepts do experience dissonance when they fail, but they experience many other negative feelings as well—due primarily to the fact that any failure for them is unpleasant. No one can deny that success brings pleasant consequences for persons with high or low self-concepts alike; that is, regardless of a person's self-concept, successful achievement (at least by Western standards) is often accompanied by such pleasant things as money, fame, acclaim, etc. But dissonance theory allows one to predict that, for people with low self-concepts, the "good feelings" aroused by the products of success will be tempered by the discomfort caused by dissonance . . . the dissonance between a low self-concept and cognitions concerning high performance.

Role theory and consistency theory together may someday prove rather invaluable to the counselor and his relationship with his client. This statement may at first appear rather odd to some readers, since upon quick reflection the two theories may not seem to have much, if anything, in common. Further consideration, however, will disclose several areas of contact between the two theories, suggesting that mutual contributions to the fields of psychology, sociology, and counseling may be possible.

The term "role theory" when used in the singular can perhaps be somewhat misleading. There are several versions of role theory, and the differences among them are severe enough to warrant the specification of which particular version one is incorporating. Role theory as presented by T. R. Sarbin will be the orientation being referred to in this paper (Sarbin, 1954). In this approach there are many concepts and basic assumptions in common with approaches of other contemporary role theorists such as Newcomb (1951), Merton (1957), Goffman (1959), and Sargent (1951).[40] The role theory approach is a very broad framework for the analysis, prediction, and control of social behavior, an aspect which should be considered important to those dealing with clients and their futures. Role theory represents the convergence of two intellectual traditions—one deriving from theoretical investigations of the growth of self and social awareness (Cooley, 1902; Mead, 1934), which emphasize cognition and its processes in social interaction; the other coming from the sociological and anthropological tradition (Durkheim, 1933; Linton, 1936, 1945), which focuses on implications of status differentiation and the division of labor within society.[41]

A role is a part assigned to a person, whether the part is in the drama of the stage or in the enactments of everyday life. A role always has its complementary role—i.e., the separate rights of a father and child. Society is composed of differentiated social positions—both formal and informal—which are often identifiable by a label or name. Integral to each position is a set of norms specifying the appropriate and expected behavior for a person occupying such a position. Behavior of a person in accordance with the expectations of the role position is termed "role enactment." Another basic concept in role theory is the cognitive organization of qualities entitled the self-conception, which refers primarily to phenomenal experience.

It has often been observed that role theory is unique in providing a theoretical framework of integration of both individual and society. Social behavior of role enactment is a function of both the individual in terms of his unique conception of self and society (or the social system) in general, in terms of the social position occupied by the person. These are extremely important affairs to be kept in mind as any psychologist or counselor attempts to aid a client. Sociologists and the sociological theory per se clearly show just how important these prementioned concepts are.

Self-perception—an individual's ability to respond differentially to his own behavior and its controlling variables—is a product of social interaction (Mead, 1934; Ryle, 1949; Skinner, 1957).[42] Verbal statements that are self-descriptive are among the most common responses comprising self-perception, and the techniques employed by the community to teach its members to make such statements would not seem to differ fundamentally from the methods used to teach interpersonal perception in general. The community, however, does face severe limitations in training the individual to make statements describing internal events to which only he has direct access. Skinner (1953, 1957) has analyzed the limited resources available to the community for training its members to "know themselves," and he has described the inescapable inadequacies of the resulting knowledge.[43]

Several studies have shown that an individual's belief and attitude statements can be manipulated by inducing him to role-play, deliver a persuasive communication, or engage in any behavior that would characteristically imply his endorsement of a particular set of beliefs (Brehm and Cohen, 1962; King and Janis, 1956; Scott, 1957, 1959).[44]

The chooser ordinarily expects himself to choose one of the best of the alternatives, at least given the information at his disposal at the time of the decision. Hence, after the chooser has made his decision, any piece of information which implies that the decision was bad (irrational) violates his expectations that he behaves rationally. It questions his ability to predict or understand his own behavior. This argument can be applied equally to the case of the person who expects himself to behave irrationally. Such a person will have his expectations about himself disconfirmed by information implying that the decision was a rational one. The ideal is that an unpleasant emotional state is aroused by attention to contra-expected information, regardless of whether that information has other implications of a predominantly desirable or undesirable nature.

Another source of discomfort said to be peculiar to the person who feels responsible for his actions and their outcomes might be stated as follows: Any information about the chosen or rejected alternatives that implies the decision was a bad one also implies that the chooser is incompetent and immoral—not capable of choosing intelligently or ethically. It is somewhat easy to confuse this source of discomfort with what was discussed earlier, where the person was allegedly disturbed because he could not understand his own behavior. In the present focus, the person is disturbed whether or not he expected himself to behave rationally.

The distinction is perhaps clearest if one examines the case of the person who expects himself to behave irrationally, or at least has a low opinion of his general ability to make decisions of the sort he is currently induced to make. Presumably, such a person does not firmly expect to find, after the decision is made, that the decision was a good one. His confidence in himself being low, he is prepared to discover that he has made a mistake. What happens when such a person attends to information implying that the decision really made was actually a poor one? It comes as no surprise; it disconfirms no strong expectations and may even confirm his expectations about himself. This does not, however, suggest that he is in no way disturbed about the irrationality of his decision. Even though he has not mispredicted his own behavior, he has nevertheless made an incompetent and immoral decision. He has brought undesirable consequences upon himself, and perhaps on others as well. This probably rearouses anxiety associated with past situations in which he has been punished for incompetent or immoral decisions.

To make the analytical decision of separation between the two sources of unpleasantness clearer, one might imagine how this person with low self-confidence feels when he attends to information implying that his decision was really a very good one. This realization is inconsistent with his expectation that he will retard the situation. Hence, it questions the understanding of his own ability, a rather frightening feeling. But this information is certainly pleasant in other respects. It permits him to, in actuality, raise his self-esteem. In such a situation this person theoretically has dissonance really aroused by his failure to confirm his expectations about himself, but at the same time he is free from the anxiety which would have resulted if he believed he had made an incompetent decision.

It is surprising that the seemingly straightforward notion of a psychological trend toward consistency comprises a host of problems which require explication. If someone should ask how such trends are conditioned by relations to the self or self-concept as a cognitive structure, he immediately faces similar complications. In spite of the apparent solidity of the term self-concept, even a mildly critical look at the literature of research and theory bearing on the topic should suffice to indicate that the solidity is illusory. Concerning conceptualization and measurement, there is no satisfactory agreement, and what traditions of measurement have emerged are not very well grounded in theory.

Phenomenological inspection yields references to the self as an actor in relation to other actors, as grounds against which experiences of an external world are figural, as maintaining identity in time, as reflexive object. Some theorists attempt to place such a phenomenal self to immediate theoretical work. However, other theorists, such as M. B. Smith, have always considered proper scientific discourse as requiring usage of what insights can be obtained from what is given phenomenally so as to frame subjective constructs.

Consider here the person's more or less stable self-concept and the transitory self-concepts perceived by him, which are evoked in the course of his transactions with the environment. "Self-percepts" will depend not only on the individual's persisting beliefs about himself (self-concept), but also upon his ongoing behavior and the informal feedback that it brings, as well as upon the treatment he is accorded by others as it varies from one situation to another. The responses evoked by self-report procedures are highly fallible means for developing inferences about either level, high or low, of construct, and the poor habit of identifying self-reports with constructs may well lead to confusion.

Within the sphere of the self-concept, one can probably distinguish a core of identity beliefs, which have persisting trans-situational relevance for a person's view of himself from the set of sub-identities which correspond to William James's notion of the person's multiple social selves—systems of belief which are bound to the major distinguishable contexts of role relations in which the person participates. One may expect pronounced individual and societal variation in the extent to which such sub-identities are differentiated with one another and from core identity.[45]

According to Smith, the psychoanalytic tradition suggests the relevance of additional distinctions mainly to simultaneously suggest the absurdity of treating the self-concept as a concrete, separate entity. One may infer that a person entertains views of himself of which he may be afraid, negative attitudes which may not be accessible to self-report; however, he also has conceptions of himself as he would like to be. In the sphere of percepts, he may reject self-regarding experiences as ego-alienated, as not pertaining to the acknowledged self.

In order to consider what the self has to do with trends toward consistency, one may commence by noting the important essence of such trends in the very constitution of the self. As consistency theories become more advanced and understandable, one can expect that one important direction in which social psychology may seek integration with personality theory is in further specifying the role of consistency-directed processes in the formation and development of the self.

Several things may now be said. First of all, the formation of a person's core identity, the differentiation of his sub-identities, and the extrusion of his negative identities would seem to be heavily influenced by trends toward consistency of two kinds: toward internal consistency with as simple a structure as possible, and toward external consistency, such that surprise and disconfirmation by new percepts are kept within tolerable bounds.[46] Heider (1958) emphasized how differentiation can be one outcome of strains toward cognitive balance; the theories derivative from Heider would seem to hold a bit more promise than dissonance theories as aids toward the understanding of differentiated structure in the self.[47]

However, consistency-seeking processes operate in conjunction with an essentially unrelated trend, a bias toward thinking as well of oneself as one can get away with. Just as Festinger's version of consistency theory weighs the discrepancy between cognitions by their importance, so the self-esteem-maximizing trend would seem also to involve a weighing by importance or centrality to one's self-concept (French and Sherwood, 1965).[48]

Involvement to the self presumably also bears upon stability and change in attitudes in ways other than those mediated by consistency-seeking processes. For example, one might consider the so-called discrepancy-involvement controversy as was summarized by McGuire in 1966. Sherif and Hovland (1961) and Sherif, Sherif, and Nebergall (1965) have claimed in the context of assimilation-contrast-judgmental theory that with stronger involvement, larger discrepancies between a person's own prior attitudinal position and the position advocated by a persuasive communication should result in decreased attitudinal change, because of the narrower latitude of acceptance which accompanies high involvement.

In overview, many authors have examined in detal the concept of self and the processes which are commonly employed in the defense and enhancement of self. Several have seemed in their individualistic ways to work toward a major revision of the consistency approach, one in which self-related processes will play a greater central role than they have yet.

Perhaps the most influential failure that forced this revisionist mood is the experimental affirmation of a difficult fact; namely, the need for maintaining internally consistent affective-cognitive structures is often subordinated to man's penchant for attempting to think well of himself and optimistically of his prospects.

Experimental evidence was already apparent, though not yet fully examined, more than fifteen years ago. One early example is Jordon's 1953 study of reactions to abstractly stated balanced and unbalanced triads. The data yielded, somewhat indirectly, that unbalanced triads are less displeasing when their content is ego-enhancing than when this is not the case. Similarly, studies by Morgan and Mortan (1944) and McGuire (1960) clarified the fact that syllogistic reasoning is often subordinated to "wish fulfillment."

The tendency to maximize expected gain and to minimize expected loss refers to (in this paper primarily) those kinds of cognitions which profess to foretell and surmise actual need-reduction or frustration in one's dealings with clients, agencies, persons in general, and events beyond the self. Many social psychologists are quite persuasive when they suggest that the maximization of gain in self-esteem and the minimization of loss in the same realm are essentials that also intrude into the cognitive processes of the individual, and which thus also turn him away from the simple pursuit of consistency in the ordering of his cognitions referring to some common object or set of related objects.

In the light of present contributions and some related recent work, it can perhaps be specified as to what are some of the important variables and processes which will have to be encompassed in the required expansion of the consistency approach to counselor-client relationship, among other things. One of these is most assuredly the individual's generalized level of self-esteem. Quite possibly it may be disclosed that where self-esteem is truly high and stable, the person is more prone to process information in ways which are keyed to consistency restoration, even when that can only be achieved at the expense of internalizing some negative judgments about the self.

The variable of ego-centrality is also likely to be confirmed as having great importance. For example, common insight suggests that when negative judgments or information about the self intrude into an otherwise favorable self-cognition system, the extent to which this will be tolerated, despite the inconsistency it arouses, may vary as an inverse function of the importance within the self-concept of the particular positive attribute that is being called into question.

Perhaps the "secret" side of the self-concept contains a few surprises. Probably as one goes from person to person within the same role category, one would find highly idiosyncratic patterns of cherished attributes. Thus, apparently similar individuals might differ considerably in the degree of ego injury associated with accepting some particular kind of negative information about the self and then having to recognize and reorganize the self-concept for it to be consistent with that information.

Some of these ideas just mentioned suggest some of the quite complex difficulties which are likely to be encountered when a development of a more precise theoretical and research approach to the integration and interaction of consistency and self-enhancement is attempted. Better techniques than are now used will probably be needed to obtain leads to the basic elements of any particular self-concept and of the pattern of interconnection between those elements. It should be kept in mind that the self as presented and represented to another may be more favorable or internally consistent than would be the case in the person's uncovered perception of himself.

Further theorizing and research in this realm will probably also have to confront one phenomologically available fact that the present investigations have, to date, slighted; that is, some individuals most of the time, and most individuals some of the time, find psychological gain in the maintenance of an image of an unattractive self along with the usual dominant attractive self. It is considered an attribute of the "normal" person that he achieve some interaction between these, and that he develop cognitive processing skills enabling him to do this. Similarly, it might serve one well to ask whether or not a negative portion of the self-concept persists because of a search to link to it man's inadequate and culpable actions. The paradoxical suggestion which might be considered here is that a positive self-concept can best be defended from the inconsistency generated by "bad" behavior if one also maintains an alternative or coexisting negative self-concept.

Bramel's paper, "Dissonance, Expectation and the Self," suggests that the tolerance for dissonance derives from a learning sequence which is frequently and universally experienced. Discrepancy between overt behavior or socially visible choice on the one hand, and private conviction, competence, or interest on the other hand, will often lead to receipt of social disapproval. Since social disapproval is a potent negative reinforcer, the ultimate effect of the frequent repetition of this sequence is that the person acquires a conditioned avoidance orientation toward situations in which such discrepancies are encountered. Thus, the person's efforts to reduce such discrepancies, whether by altering his private convictions or his estimates of his own competence and rationality, are ultimately derived from his need for social approval.[49]

There is a host of necessary and important topics which could be discussed and incorporated at this point. The practicality of time and length have caused such discussion to be omitted. Suffice it to say that to omit themes such as "dissonance reduction in the behaviorists," "the problem of motivation in consistency," "dissonance without awareness," "cognitive dissonance and the control of human behavior," "commitment," and the like, almost seems to make a paper of this scope somewhat incomplete. Any psychologist or counselor, as well as any layman, should clearly understand the problems with which he may be confronted as he himself either consciously or unknowingly manipulates or guides the lives of others. People lie, deceive, fear, pretend, safeguard, escape, and defend themselves almost automatically even against those persons and factors that may be genuinely directed toward their process, growth, understanding, and actualization in general. Perhaps Freud hit upon something more phenomenal in this area of psychology than the social sciences are currently recognizing. At any rate, however, psychotherapy, counseling, and even everyday discussion among friends should perhaps be built around a better understanding and realization of what is truly transpiring within the lonely, small, and distant world of an individual who is unhappy enough, friendless enough, unorganized enough, so as to feel alienated from those around him.

In this chapter several themes have been touched upon regarding aggression. A brief synopsis of aggression was discussed as well as some of the primary theories surrounding the origin of, the different types of, the attitudes toward, and the possible causes of aggression.

At this time criminal aggression in particular will be discussed, since currently it is this type or aspect of aggression which seems to be of most concern to the majority of the American people.

Criminality and Aggressive Behavior

It is an accepted fact by the vast majority of the people of this country, professionals and laymen alike, that crime is increasing at a cancerous rate all over the civilized world. This fact by no means excludes even rural America, where the crime rate, all other things being equal, is on the upswing, and geometrically so when compared to urban crime. People are becoming more and more fearful of dealing with one another, and this fact itself seems to have a positive correlation with respect to the further increase of crime.

War has always existed in one way or another in civilized and uncivilized, ancient and modern-day cultures and societies alike; and so, quite naturally, the questions arise, "Why are we violent? Why have we always been violent?"

Although there is no general agreement with regard to the above questions, it is becoming more and more evident with each and every passing day that if something is not done to control this social menace, self-destruction seems almost inevitable for most, if not all, of the human population.

Americans have always been very proud of the fact that to many foreign nations they have long been considered "children lovers and family people." Yet child abuse and wife-beating run rampant in America, even between two people who continuously will avow their love for each other.

One half of all murders in this country result from family affairs.[50] Sixty percent of police reports are filed under "domestic disputes."[51] Children die more from being beaten than from leukemia, accidents, and muscular dystrophy combined.[52] Nine out of ten murders are those of the same race and nationality, and three out of four murders are between people who know each other and who are under the influence of alcohol.[53]

The tremendous increase of violent crime is in its second decade. Unfortunately, violence is concentrated on those in society we care least about. As previously mentioned, people who are fearful are more often than not the victims of violence, and the billions of dollars spent for material, manpower, and crisis reaction programs have not reduced crime.

Many theories have tried to explain the cause of crime as a result of drug abuse, alcohol abuse (if you so choose to separate the two), the influence of the media, and/or the influx of newcomers. One American rural county, Adams County, explains its recent homicide occurrences as a result of all of the above-mentioned aspects. The Adams County sheriff stated that for decades there were no murders, rapes, or manslaughter assaults in Adams County, and that during the past five years, hideous, intermittent murders are causing fear and confusion among the county's population.[54]

Other theorists suggest that crime is not so much the result of forces outside the individual, but more so by innate, biological, hereditary-type chemical imbalances within certain parts of the brain.

Over the years innumerous theories documenting the causation of criminal violence have materialized, and each apparently points the finger of blame at different areas of either society or the individual. And so, theories have spotlighted as the major cause of violent and criminal behavior either the educational system in America, the Criminal Justice System, the media, the economic conditions at any given point in time, the types of laws, the manner in which the laws are enforced by the police, the corrections systems, the positions of the stars and planets, the chemistry within the individual, a changing, growing society. Theories have also traced crime to a changing, regressing society, religious techniques, sexual buildup, alcohol and drug abuse, and/or almost any other conceivable excuse which can be given to help explain away the overall immature behavior of a people who have not yet learned "how to think," but rather "what to think"; who have not yet learned to think for themselves and to think constructively, but rather are persuaded to look around and see what others are doing and wanting before each decides what he or she wants to do.

For one thing, to speak about cause and effect under any circumstance can be a very dangerous thing. For example, to say that criminal and violent behavior is the result of drug abuse does little more than raise the following questions: Why would a person abuse drugs? Do the drugs create the violence within an otherwise tranquil person, or do they only bring forward the violence that is dormant within? How come all drug abusers do not become violent?

Another example: to say that crime and violence are caused or even abetted through the mass media also does little but raise such questions as: Isn't the media only a composite of the people who are part of that population? Does the mass media direct the people with regard to what they will be entertained by, or do the people dictate what the media will project? Are people intelligent and aware enough to ignore what they feel is harmful to them through a learning, or, perhaps more specifically, a brainwashing process, or are they totally nothing more than a product of the environment? And so on.

One thing is for sure: abetters of violence and, more specifically, violent crime, are prejudice, from broken homes, and poor and/or unstable economic conditions.[55] These ingredients seem to have a significant impact over whether drugs (alcohol included) will be abused or misused, how the people will tend to think, how people relate to one another, particularly in a problem-solving situation; how people respond (act and react) to the persuasions and hidden insinuations of the mass media, and, in general, how individuals feel about themselves and their placement, or misplacement, in society.

Violent television programs, theater films, and sports are among the most popular pastimes of the American people. Even cartoons oftentimes express extreme violence in one way or another. If the entertainment is not of a violent nature, it simply does not become too popular.

Perhaps violent scenes or stories are as popular as they are because they represent occurrences which people do not normally see in their everyday lives. Perhaps people want to experience, see, and feel what is new and different as a result of curiosity and the learning process, which can be stated otherwise as the basic desire of man to explore the unfamiliar.

One movie producer stated that "we try to reach the greater mass of the public more so emotionally than intellectually."[56] Margaret Meade, renowned sociologist, stated, "Put something peaceful on and the people turn off the set."[57]

One member of the TV Communications Association stated, "We wish to generate fear through the mass media so that we might eventually gain more control of the people through authority."[58] This last statement, in reference to the control of people, is not too far from the general belief and strategy of Adolph Hitler. The problem, then, is real; the consequences possibly fatal.

If aggression is examined in different cultures, one will find little evidence that it is universal. Such societies as the Tasaday of the Philippine Islands, the Arapesh of New Guinea, the Lepchas of Sikkim, and the Ituri pygmies of the Congo are reported by several researchers to show absolutely no overt signs of violence whatsoever. However, it is true that there have been few enough "Appollonian" peoples, as Ruth Benedict has called members of nonviolent cultures, so that it could be argued that the nonaggressive cultures are in some sense merely mutations, exceptions that still do not in actuality dispute the rule, which states that man is innately aggressive. Nevertheless, even though it is true that the above-mentioned so-called nonviolent tribes constitute only a small portion of humanity, to date there still is lacking enough positive scientific evidence to show that these groups are in any way genetically atypical. In fact, on the contrary, one might just as easily conclude from existing research material that the mere existence of such nonviolent peoples indicates that humans are not necessarily aggressive; that humans can learn nonviolent behavior and practices from those who live them out on a daily basis. In brief, "neither the evidence from animal or psychophysiological research nor from psychoanalytic and anthropological research justifies the conclusion that as a species we are all the carriers of violent impulses which are bound to expression."[59] In fact, a major objection to the notion of instinct yet exists, in that it is not subject to empirical testing, and that there is no morally acceptable way to empirically prove that any complex behavior is an instinct in humans. Even animal researchers have backed off from their original definition of instinct. No longer is an instinct believed to be totally an internal impulse to engage in certain behavior. In most circumstances external environmental requirements must also be met before an "instinct" is expressed. Tinbergen has gone so far as to suggest that instinct be replaced by the term "fixed-action pattern" to indicate that the behavior is not spontaneously emitted by the organism, but is most typically elicited by external stimulation in conjunction with some internal state of the organism.[60] Since, then, one of the rules of science is to assume that nothing is "true" unless the evidence indicates that it is not false, it seems safest at this point to suggest that humans are born with the capacity and potential for learning to behave violently and/or, of course, peacefully.

It might do well here, in order to provide more structure and continuity to the discussions to follow, to establish a general mode of aggression—a simple model of aggression or aggressive behavior to serve as a guideline for examining various instances of human aggression. Let it first be understood, however, that the terms violence and aggression in this paper are being considered synonymously, as they are by Jeffrey H. Goldstein, and defined as "behavior of which the intent is the physical or psychological injury of another,"[61] and that "aggressive behavior used by someone to achieve a personal goal, such as wealth or power, and which may be perceived by the actor as justified (or even non-aggressive) is a primary cause of aggressive and criminal behavior of others."[62] This definition, however, does not intend to insinuate that there are not forms of socially acceptable aggression or anger, for example.

Aggressive behavior is complex, based on any number of simultaneously existent and coexistent factors. If an aggressive act is to occur, it would seem inevitable that there should also be some impetus to aggress, inhibitions against aggressing to be overpowered, and an appropriate situation at hand, in terms of the opportunity and ability to aggress as well as the availability of an acceptable target.[63] If these aspects are accepted as somewhat influential mechanisms of every, or perhaps most, acts of violence, then any model of aggressive behavior must incorporate these factors within it.

It is proposed here that two sets of opposing tendencies (Ref: cognitive dissonance) operate in any potentially aggressive situation (i.e., tendencies to aggress and tendencies to not aggress).[64] Whether or not a person aggresses, the behavior elicited is a product of this conflict. Which tendency will be expressed is not the vital issue here; rather, the vital issue is the understanding that the decision of whether or not to behave violently in any particular situation depends upon the relative strength of the two opposing forces of aggression and non-aggression.

Jeffrey Goldstein, as will this paper, divides the pro- and anti-aggression factors into long-term factors and situational factors:

> Long-term factors are those which are relatively enduring, or personality characteristics of the individual, such as his or her norms, attitudes and values toward aggression, prior experience with aggression, and knowledge of and ability to use aggressive or non-aggressive strategies in interpersonal disputes. Likewise, in any given instance, there are situational idiosyncracies which may facilitate or inhibit aggressive behavior. These immediate, situational factors often play a prominent role in any act of violence.[65]

The main force behind enduring factors toward aggression is, of course, the socialization process which a child from any society must experience. As this process is taking place, the child gradually acquires a set of beliefs, norms, attitudes, values and expectations about aggressive behavior; and it is these long-term norms, attitudes, beliefs, values, and expectations which are usually most influentially acquired through selective reinforcement from, and the examples set by, one's parents, peers, family, and teachers, each of whom have also been socialized in a particular manner. These long-term norms, values, etc., are relatively stable and usually remain basically unchanged during an individual's lifetime. There are two basic reasons for the persistence exhibited by such attitudes, norms, etc. First of all, a person will usually choose to be with people who share his norms and values (Ref: cognitive dissonance). Second, once one acquires certain norms, etc., he is almost psychologically forced to organize subsequent behavior and beliefs that support that normative framework (Ref: cognitive dissonance).

Situational factors which facilitate aggression are, however, also very important regarding one's decision to behave aggressively or nonaggressively. The importance of these factors becomes increasingly important as one understands the most violent of individuals. Not even these people are perpetually in a state of violent acting out, no more than would the most passive among us *never* be persuaded to behave aggressively under certain circumstances. It is these circumstances which diminish normal inhibitions against aggressing, such as the presence of friends and relatives, familiar surroundings, victims associated in the actor's mind with aggression, alcohol, certain drugs, the presence and availability of a weapon, and an environment which would abet the anonymity of the aggressor and his actions. If a particular factor either momentarily raises one's tendency to aggress or inhibits one's restraints against aggressing, it is a situational, pro-agression factor.

Although people do learn which situations, targets, and means are appropriate for aggression, they at the same time learn which situations, targets, and means are inappropriate. One example might be that it is more admissible for a man to hit a man of equal build and age than it is for a young man to hit a woman, child, or senior citizen. Aggressive situations would include, for example, barrooms, public streets, vacant lots; non-aggressive locations include churches, private homes, offices of high public figures, etc. In short, then, it would be safe to say that an actor who aggresses against an old woman in a church would be behaving more aggressively than one who engages in the same physical act against a thirty-year-old man in a barroom. The main reason behind such a deduction is that the former has to violate more social taboos and overcome more resistance than the latter.

Treating pro- and anti-aggression systems independently becomes meaningful when one realizes that there may be factors which encourage nonaggressive behavior, which are not simply related to the absence of factors which encourage aggression. Briefly, people may learn positive forms of social interaction rather than mere inactivity as an alternative to violence.[66] One person may deal with interpersonal conflict by behaving non-aggressively because of the belief that disputes ought to be resolved by peaceful arbitration. Thus, not acting aggressively does not mean precisely the same thing as acting nonaggressively. Even the most violent people tend to be nonviolent in many, if not most, circumstances. This realization brings up the intricacies involving situational factors which facilitate nonaggression. Major situational factors which are likely to reduce aggression are the presence of a potentially punishing agent—such as a policeman or parent—an unfamiliar environment, unfamiliar potential victims, easy identifiability of the aggressor and his actions, and the presence of non-aggressive others.

Since aggression is viewed here as the result of a conflict (Ref: cognitive dissonance), the probability of aggressive behavior is calculated by considering the ratio of pro-aggression elements—both situational and long-term—to anti-aggression elements, situational as well as long-term.

Interestingly, the belief that aggression occurs because a variety of norms and values are in conflict with one another is quite different from the notion proposed by a number of sociologists—most notably, Emile Durkheim—who view aggression and anti-social behavior to be the result of too few norms (a state referred to as anomie). However, returning to the premise proposed by this paper— namely, that aggression (also depression) is the result of conflict—it is simultaneously proposed

> that the more conflict present in any given situation, the longer it will take to decide whether to act aggressively or not. Although very few studies have measured the time it takes to respond aggressively, it is expected to be longer in high conflict situations than in low. This may be due to the need to consider more elements and to resolve the conflict more fully prior to behaving overtly. In addition, when conflict is high, there will be more postbehavior cognitive consequences of the fact. When there are both many and strong reasons to act aggressively combined with many and potent reasons for not acting aggressively, conflict is high and the mental work required to resolve the conflict in the actor's mind is considerable. Once the decision has been made to act aggressively, the intensity of the act will be stronger than if conflict were less. It is proposed that this is because of the need to justify one's actions, and there is less justification for violence in high than in low conflict situations. Thus, high conflict situations lead us to the following hypotheses: (a) the more conflict present in the system, the longer it takes for the individual to act; (b) the more conflict in the system, the more intense the aggression; (c) the more conflict, the more cognitive consequences of the aggression, such as in reevaluation of the situation, the action, or the victim.[67]

Even though it is true that any person's level of aggression is likely to increase or decrease depending on the circumstances, some people are more likely to act aggressively than are others. It becomes of significant importance, then, to examine the degree to which individuals differ in their levels and frequencies of violence. What will be examined in the following pages of this chapter is a number of factors, most of them influential during childhood and adolescence, which are positively related to violence in adult life. Among these will be the learning of aggression and aggression-related norms and attitudes from peers, parents, and impersonal models. Impersonal models for learning aggressive norms include violent figures, whether they be real or fictitious, especially those portrayed in the mass media (e.g., sports, entertainment, advertising, and the like).

"All theoretical models of aggression assume that aggressive behavior is, to some degree, acquired. The disagreement among theorists lies primarily in the importance ascribed to learning as a determinant of aggression, and in the kinds of aggression and aggressive behavior which are assumed to be influenced by past learning."[68]

Learning theorists make a distinction between classical learning and operant learning or conditioning. Classical conditioning pairs some neutral object with an object that normally causes a particular response. After repeated pairings, the neutral object is then capable of formulating the same response. Classical learning (conditioning) was first brought to major recognition through the classical studies and research of Pavlov (1849-1936).[69]

Operant conditioning, which is most often associated with B. F. Skinner of Harvard University, but which can clearly be traced to psychologist E. L. Thorndike (1874-1949), represents a type of learning process by which rewards presented to a responsive subject serve to strengthen the response and increase the likelihood that it will occur again, while punishments presented after a response decrease the probability that the response will be repeated.

Norms, values, beliefs, attitudes, and expectations regarding aggression can be learned, as aforementioned, from one's parents, and later from teachers and peers, through classical and operant processes and imitation. If aggression is discussed by one's parents, for example, with positive overtones, then the concept expressed will be perceived as positive and thus accepted by the child.[70]

However, children are not usually provided with indiscriminate rewards for aggressive behavior, nor is aggression generally spoken of in the home in uniformly, consistently favorable terms. It is more likely that the parents and "significant others" may reward in some manner aggression that is directed toward particular targets, such as Puerto Ricans ("spicks") or Blacks ("niggers"). Such discriminations have two major consequences. First, the child may perceive the actions of others as inconsistent with regard to those situations when aggression is considered to be appropriate; or those who do reward the child may, in fact, be inconsistent in their own behavior. It is such inconsistency—more so than even consistent irrational or negative behavior, particularly from parents—which is frequently interpreted as a cause of aggressive behavior among children.[71] Second, the distinctions made between targets made by others, while they may be to some extent adopted by the child, are likely to be rather fragile and tenuous; that is, the child may be cognitively unable to formulate or maintain the fine distinctions that adults might make with regard to targets of aggression. Therefore, so-called "acceptable" behaviors of aggression directed toward, for example, "that ignorant Pole," may generally channel aggression to other targets, such as members of other American born or religious minorities. However, it is more often true than not that the learned targets of aggression definitely defined as acceptable will more often serve as victims than other targets to which the learning generalizes.[72]

A well-known study by Sears, Maccoby, and Levin[73] examined child-rearing practices and children's aggressive behavior. Nearly four hundred mothers of kindergarten youngsters were interviewed concerning their use of disciplinary measures, the acceptance or rejection of their children's aggressive behavior, feeding, and sexual behavior patterns, and their children's expression of aggression toward peers, siblings, and parents. Among the major findings of the study was that the use of physical punishment by parents was positively related to the amount of aggression shown by the children. High and severe punishment, when paired with high permissiveness toward the children's behavior, was even more strongly associated with children's aggression. More than one-third of the girls and over two-fifths of the boys rated as highly aggressive were the offspring of parents who heavily relied on physical punishment as a disciplinary measure, and who were also highly permissive.[74] Several questions, then, can be raised concerning the use of physical

punishment in general in child-rearing. According to traditional learning theory, if a child is punished for aggressive behavior he should then be expected to refrain from aggressing in the future. Yet, the results of research on punishment and children's aggression oftentimes disclose that punishment only begets aggression.

According to Bandura,[75] children learn not only from direct reward and punishment, but also from observation. For example, it would take a child considerably longer to learn a language if it had to rely totally on rewards and punishment for correct and incorrect verbalization; instead, each is able to imitate the verbal speech patterns of those around him.

Again according to Bandura and others,[76] a child will learn behavior that it observes in others, providing that neither the others nor the child-observer is punished for that behavior.

"In the case of a parent spanking a child for behaving aggressively. . . . It is not surprising, then, that aggressive parents have aggressive offspring."[77]

Similar imitation and modeling as that just described above can occur also via other influential forces, besides the parents, within a society. One such force is the behavioral and moral code depicted by others in society at large. Such general social norms are portrayed in the behavior of those real and fictitious people with whom the child comes in contact in actual everyday living—in stories, in books, through sports, the theater, and in television, to name a few.

The process of selective reinforcement is one way in which children acquire aggressive and nonaggressive behaviors. Imitation, a more subtle process, also contributes to a child's aggressive behavior patterns. Children oftentimes have demonstrated that they will identify themselves with, and use as models, those whom they love, admire, or even fear. The child copies many modes of behavior, particularly those of its parents, that have even been, at least overtly, discouraged. In other words, children may well at times imitate more what we *do* than what we *say* they should do. Parents who beat their children for being violent often do not realize that they are teaching the child, by hitting him, that violence is necessary in order to get others to behave as you wish.

A child learns much of his aggressive behavior from parents, friends and other adults, but what each child is encouraged to learn may depend on the child's gender. Culture is not co-educational; there are separate curricula for boys and girls. From early infancy boys and girls receive different treatment from their parents and from society. For example, we encourage vigorous physical activity by boys, and dainty, coquettish behavior in girls. A boy who will not fight risks being labelled a "sissy" by his peers; a girl who engages in physical aggression goes beyond the acceptable tomboy role.[78]

The paradox lies in our own ambivalence about the value of aggression, including its more extreme violent forms. Many of us secretly admire the two-fisted, pistol-packing male who is ready to take the law into his own hands when the situation calls for it. And some of us openly admire the violent archetype of the American dream. Eric Hofler stated, as a member of the President's Commission on the Causes and Prevention of Violence, that we need strong men who love a fight, who when they get up in the morning spit on their hands and ask "whom will I kill today?"[79]

Although direct reinforcement is generally initiated and most intense as it relates to the parents of a particular child, one of the remaining and most important behavior persuaders is the actions and motives of adults on television and in the movies. Studies on the subject basically support the idea that most children watch TV for two hours or more per day, not counting weekends. At this rate, by the time the youngster is sixteen, he or she will have spent more time watching television than learning in school. Advertisers, and the psychologists behind them, spend literally hundreds of millions of dollars each year realizing that TV has a powerful effect on people's attitudes and behavior—the young viewers being the most vulnerable. It is not difficult to ascertain the effects of such a pervasive medium on the social development of the youth of this country, and it does not take much in-depth research to disclose that children easily identify with the behavioral patterns of the games (e.g., sports) that society condones.

In the realm of human aggression, more research has been conducted on the effects of violence in the mass media than on practically any other single topic. Following twenty years of research, controversy and debate still rage over the effects of portrayed violence on aggressive behavior.

Since science is a descriptive enterprise rather than a proscriptive one, it can only describe reality as it is at present and in many instances predict future realities; it cannot, however, involve itself with what reality *ought* to be like.

R. M. Liebert has summarized a great deal of the pertinent research that aids in the explanation of what evidence actually is with respect to media violence:

> This data suggest consistently that children are exposed to a heavy dose of violence on television. It is also clear that they can and do retain some of the aggressive behaviors which they see, and are often able to reproduce them. Differences in recall as a function of age are in the expected direction (better recall with increasing age). Differences in recall as a function of content are less clearly understood, but violent content appears to be learned and remembered at least as well as non-violent fare. . . . Punishment to an aggressive model leads children to avoid reproduction of exemplary behavior, but does not prevent learning or subsequent performance under more favorable circumstances. . . . It is important to note that the correlational results, while generally consistent, point to a moderate (rather than strong) relationship between watching television violence and subsequent aggressive attitudes and behavior.[80]

In a 1965 study by Albert Bandura, sixty-six nursery school children were exposed to one of three five-minute films on a TV console:

> In all three films an adult enacted a series of verbal and physical attacks on a plastic Bobo doll. One group of children observed the model rewarded following the aggression with candy and soft drinks. A second group of children saw the model punished

following the aggression with spanking and verbal rebukes. A third group of children saw only the model's aggressive behavior with no rewarding or punishing consequences. The children were then allowed to play for ten minutes in a room which contained, among other toys, a Bobo doll. During the play period, the children's aggressive behaviors were observed and recorded. Following the free-play period, children were told that they would receive fruit juices and picture booklets if they would imitate the behavior that they had seen in the film. The children's aggression during the free-play period is an index of the extent to which the films influenced "spontaneous" aggression, while their behavior during the last phase of the study represents the extent to which they learned and could reproduce the aggressive behavior they had seen in the film. Spontaneous aggression was greatest in the groups which had seen the model rewarded and which had seen the aggression without any reinforcing consequences; it was least in the group which had seen the model punished for aggression. Thus, punishment may serve to inhibit spontaneous aggression among children-observers. When asked to imitate the aggression they had seen, all three groups of children were equally able to duplicate the model's aggressive performance. Thus, learning of aggression took place regardless of whether the model was rewarded, punished, or neither.

The implications of this study are many and varied. They indicate that children are capable of learning what they see, regardless of the presence of rewards or punishments. Second, the results suggest that children are likely to imitate the aggressive behavior they observe in the mass media providing that the aggressor was not punished for his or her actions. Finally, the results indicate that, contrary to many theories of learning, new forms of behavior can be acquired in the absence of rewards.[81]

The evidence for a reduction of aggression following observation of violent behavior seems to be far outweighed by the innumerous studies that report that the observation of violence serves to stimulate aggression.

Jeffrey Goldstein together with Ralph Rosnow and Tamas Raday of Temple University conducted a media-aggression study in four countries—namely, Canada, Italy, England, and the United States—using a natural, non-laboratory research setting with full-length films.[82] Among the films shown were *Clockwork*

Orange and *Straw Dogs*, which represented aggressive films; *The Decameron*, which was arousing but not aggressive; and *Fiddler on the Roof* and *Living Free*, which were neither arousing nor aggressive—in other words, neutral. Adult males were interviewed either before or after they had viewed one of these films. The interview was designed to assess the viewer's level of punitiveness, which was used as an index of aggressiveness. The results indicated that there was a statistically significant increase in the aggressiveness measure after the viewing of an aggressive film in all four countries, while there was a general decrease in aggressiveness after viewing a non-arousing, non-aggressive film. Sexual films had no appreciable effect on observers' levels of punitiveness. A study such as this indicates as a whole the following: (a) aggressive films have an effect on viewers' levels of aggression; (b) the results are not peculiar to Americans; and (c) the increase in aggressiveness was due to the aggressive content of the film rather than to its arousing qualities.

It has often been suggested that the influence of mass-media violence is greatest for young children who are unable to distinguish reality from fantasy. The research on this question, however, fails to support this contention. Even while recognizing that violence on television is fictional and staged, adults too have been found to become more aggressive following exposure to media violence.[83]

It has also been argued that whatever influence televised violence has, it is short-lived. Again, the research indicates that, to the contrary, the effects of exposure to media violence may persist for at least four to five months.[84]

One important abstract behavioral style related to aggression is an individual's impulsivity. As Mischel states, "Even the most simple, most primitive steps in socialization require learning to defer one's impulses and to express them only under special circumstances of time and place, as seen in toilet training. Similarly, enormously complex chains of deferred gratification are required for people to achieve the delayed rewards provided by our culture's social system and institutions."[85]

The inability to delay gratification (impulsivity) is both

directly and indirectly related to aggression and criminality.[86] As Mischel notes, many rewards provided by society require the ability to postpone immediate but small rewards for long-term but larger rewards.

In addition to instituting their own socially deviant means to social goals, highly impulsive people are also likely to react with aggression to interpersonal difficulties. Violence is a tempting and impulsive solution to interpersonal problems. It is tempting because it has the effect of reducing the complexities and subtleties normally found in human problems to a simple contest of strength and agility.

An important experiment by Bandura and Mischel demonstrates that impulsivity can be learned through processes of imitation and modeling.[87] Children with little tendency to delay gratification were exposed to a model who, when given a choice between an immediate small reward and a future larger one, chose the latter. Children who tended to delay gratification were exposed to a model who chose the immediate small reward. Both groups of children, when tested following exposure to the respective models, showed significant changes. Low delay of gratification observers became better able to delay immediate gratification, while children initially high in delay of gratification tended to become lower. These results suggest that the kinds of postponement and planning for rewards demonstrated by parents, and others to whom the child is exposed, will influence the child's own such tendencies.

In particular, the child's expectations of and trust in others influences his impulsivity. To the extent that the child has trust in others, there is a tendency to imitate modeled delay of gratification; when trust in others is absent, the child will tend to be impulsive and low in the ability to postpone immediate rewards.[88]

Crook has noted that "the behavior of crowds watching 'conventionally' competitive sports often indicates the arousal of aggressive attitudes rather than their happy sublimation. . . . The wanton destruction of train interiors by British football team supporters . . . reveals a release of social tensions in what would appear to be highly convivial surroundings. Indeed, the holding of major sporting events is often manageable only when effective rules of crowd control are operative."[89]

As seen in the studies on mass-media violence, observers tend to learn and imitate the violence they witness on the movie and TV screens, and it might be reasonable to expect that being exposed to violence in sports, like watching it on TV, tends to increase the likelihood of observers becoming either aggressive or at least more so aggressive than at the onset.

However, there have been a number of researchers of human aggression who have suggested, to the contrary, that participation in and observation of aggressive sports serve as a safety valve, which tends to reduce participants' and observers' levels of aggression. Among those who have proposed that catharsis of aggression occurs have been William James, Freud, Ardrey, and Lorenz. Anthony Storr has gone as far as to say that "rivalry between nations in sports can do nothing but good."[90]

There are the two above extreme positions—namely, increase in violence versus decrease in violence following violent exposure —as well as several intermediate theoretical positions. Based on the frustration-aggression theory of Dollard and his Yale colleagues, it would be expected that watching aggression would lead to an increase in aggression only for those observers who were in some way frustrated.

Following the study of Bandura discussed earlier, one might consider that watching a team lose a game in an aggressive sport is in some way perceived as a punishment for the observers' or participants' behavior, while watching a team win a game is perceived as a reward for their behavior. This might tend to suggest that aggressive observers, for example, who have rooted for their teams to victory, will be more aggressive after the game than before it. It should be noted here, though, that if one relates the same circumstances to Festinger's theory of cognitive dissonance, a different conclusion can be drawn, namely, that to put all that aggressive energy into a losing team would create much dissonance and would have to be accounted for either by continuing the aggressiveness (because the team lost) or by simply stating that it was not really aggression after all, but rather just plain fun.

Dissonance theory predicts that when people find themselves doing something, and they have neither been rewarded adequately for doing it nor threatened with dire consequences for not doing it, they will find internal reasons for their behavior. The need for people, particularly Western people, to believe that they are kind and decent can lead them to say and do unkind and indecent things; can lead them into an unconscious decision to be cruel. For example, after the National Guard killed four students at Kent State University, several rumors were quickly spread stating that the slain girls were pregnant, so that their deaths in actuality spared their families great shame. There also were rumors that the four students were unbathed.

Keith Davis and Edward Jones demonstrated the need to justify cruelty. They persuaded students to help them with an experiment, in the course of which the volunteers had to tell another student that he was dull, untrustworthy, and shallow. Volunteers managed to convince themselves that they did not like the victim of their cruel analysis. They actually found him less attractive than they did before they had to criticize him.[91]

Similarly, David Glass persuaded a group of subjects to deliver electric shocks to others. The subjects again decided that the victim really deserved the cruelty, rating him in general as mean and ignorant. As Glass proceeded further, he concluded that a subject with high self-esteem was most likely to derogate the victim. Ironically enough, Glass further concluded that a person thinking he is a *good guy* is precisely why he decides that the person he has hurt is nothing more than bad, deserving exactly what he got. On the other hand, individuals with low self-esteem do not feel the need to justify their behavior and thus can comfortably derogate their victims; it is consonant for such persons to believe that they have behaved badly—"worthless people like me do unkind things."[92]

And so, Elliot Aronson, on the basis of his own experiments, reformulated Festinger's original theory in terms of the self-concept. That is, dissonance is most powerful when self-esteem is threatened. Aronson's research results also had him conclude that the students who had had their self-esteem attacked, cheated far more than those who had received positive, constructive feedback about themselves. Aronson concluded that "it may well be that low self-esteem is a critical antecedent of criminal or cruel behavior."[93]

William Goode once stated that "many people are capable of homicide or assault whose earlier experiences could not be distinguished from those of the law abiding."[94] This consideration introduces what have been termed the situational factors associated with aggression. The situational approach to aggression and crime assumes that, among people who have learned at least some aggressive behaviors, personality and early childhood experiences play only a partial role in the causation of violent acts. Of utmost importance, then, in aggression are factors present in the situation immediately preceding the act.[95] Among the most important of these factors are motives, victim-offender relationship, availability of a weapon, environmental factors, such as the time of day, the time of year, etc., and the abuse or misuse of outside agents, such as drugs. If, for example, positive interaction between two people is fairly intense, then negative interaction, as say, during an argument, will be equally, or perhaps even more intense. A possible explanation of this occurrence is that the intensity of interaction between any two people is relatively constant, while the quality of the effect, either positive or negative, changes with the circumstances.

The paradox of inordinate amounts of violence being perpetrated against friends and relatives can be resolved by recognizing the need of the aggressor to justify his or her actions (Ref: cognitive dissonance), usually by devaluing the victim.

Melvin Lerner has proposed a theory on the psychological devaluation of such victims of circumstances, which he calls the "just world phenomenon."[96] This theory suggests that people have a need to believe that events in the world are just and meaningful. If a good or evil thing is observed as having happened to others, there is a tendency to look for reasons, for explanations; and when people look hard enough, they will find or fabricate them. An experiment by Jones and Aronson found, for example, that the more respectable the victim of a rape, the greater the fault attributed to the woman for the incident.[97]

At some point the act of arguing or aggressing may become autonomous and done simply for its own sake. It just may be that highly intense verbal or physical assaults become self-reinforcing and may have an almost hypnotic effect, wherein the actor loses awareness of his or her surroundings. One thing is for sure, though, and that is that a considerable amount and degree of violent crime has been committed by first offenders; people who were in the wrong place, with the wrong people, and under the wrong circumstances.

The issues discussed in this chapter are issues important to practically every society where aggression is a social factor. What has been suggested as vital for violence in America is also considered crucial for violence practically anywhere on earth.

The Yanomamo, for example, are one of the few unacculturated indigenous groups of large size remaining in South America. Known also as the Shiriana and Waica, this tribe has a warfare pattern undisturbed by contact with national populations and the influx of firearms. These people engage in chronic and bitter raiding, in which lives are lost and captives taken. The Yanomamo are an exceptionally fierce, warlike people, oftentimes enacting turbulent and pointless violence within and between their own communities.

The Yanomamo number below 15,000 and live in widely scattered villages, seldom larger than 200 inhabitants, with little conflict or contact with the outside world. Despite the fact that their agriculture is prosperous and their game prolific, the hostilities between their villages are not only savage and murderous, but almost unceasing as well. If a village can find no evidence of an attack by another, then it may find a less tangible reason for aggression; it may claim that disease, for example, among its members is the result of sorcery by the other village. Wars and duels are a part of their lives sustained only by the cultivating and harvesting of their food crops.

The Dani tribe, with a population of approximately 75,000, live in New Guinea. Their main activity is warfare; however, unlike other aggressive tribes, their casualties are low. War is caused by the need to revenge a murdered man so that his ghost may rest in peace. As the enemy, a neighboring tribe called the Wittaia, has the same reason for its aggression, the cycle is never-ending. If a man is badly wounded by a spear thrust, small cuts are made in his stomach to let the "black blood" escape.

In contrast to both of the above-mentioned tribes is the Warao tribe. These people act out some of the most aggressive rituals not only in Venezuela where they reside, but throughout the world. However, their violence is bloodless and painless, usually released by loud screaming and the calling of obscenities and insults, or through striking at the shields and other protective armor of the supposed enemy.

Perhaps the most interesting and direct study of nonaggressive behavior is that which was carried out by Robert Dentan among the Semai of Malaya. Dentan spent well over a year with these people and was overwhelmed by the emphasis on nonviolence in their culture.

The Semai live in the hills and mountains of Central Malaya. They are a small group of slash-and-burn agriculturists who have recently given up a hunting and gathering existence (although they still hunt somewhat) and have retreated under pressure of a more culturally advanced Malaya. According to Dentan, they number about 12,000.

Interpersonal relations among the Semai are focused around the concept of "punan." This concept involves the idea that to make someone unhappy, especially by frustrating his desires, will increase the probability of the victim having an accident which will injure him physically. With punan at work, it is therefore unnecessary for the Semai to inflict harm on one another.

Adolescent Criminality
and Aggression

In 1973 approximately three thousand youths under sixteen years of age were arrested in New York State for burglary charges alone; in 1975, more than six thousand arrests; and the rate still has an upward trend, more so than can be accounted for by the increase in population. In 1970, again in New York State, nineteen youths under sixteen years of age were arrested for murder; in 1975, more than fifty were arrested for the same, also with the rate yet increasing. Fifteen percent of all street crime is enacted by persons under the age of sixteen. At least two-thirds of those arrested were rearrested, and one-third were reinstitutionalized. Juvenile delinquents, in general, appear to have little remorse, much hostility toward authority, and most often come from one-parent families. Their victims are mostly from the senior citizen population, and many have difficulty being anything but aggressive whenever their time is not almost totally and continuously occupied.[98]

Frustrated and cynical police officers say that the protection of society is grossly neglected, and that, if they had the opportunity to do so, they could offer case after case to prove such.[99]

It is a known fact that most juveniles who have committed an offense against society go untouched by the law. For one thing, many cases are handled and crushed at the Family Court Intake level, and even if a case does reach the courtroom, more often than not it is dismissed or grossly delayed as a result of a missing or frightened witness, frustrated or frightened complainants, missing or unprovable information, overloaded calendars, loopholes in the law, a technicality regarding the rights of the youngster and/or overcrowding in reformatory facilities, thus forcing the judge to release a particular youth at any given time.[100]

On top of everything else, in New York, for example, the first crime a youth commits after the age of sixteen is considered a first offense, regardless of the youth's record before age sixteen.[101]

It is obvious that the American Criminal Justice System, and most systems in this country, is reactionary rather than actionary; if a problem does not appear to pose a direct, personal, immediate threat to the majority of the people, no one is really all that concerned about it.[102]

The needs of the youngsters and the protection of society are not being taken care of. The juvenile must be reached before he becomes antisocial and violent. These are points of view pretty much agreed upon by the vast majority of the American public, particularly those professionals and laymen involved directly with the responsibility of deterring crime and overall fear in this country. The remaining questions basically then revolve around how this long-sought-after, difficult-to-obtain goal might be somehow reached.

Briefly, the general attitude of the taxpaying public toward such issues as those just mentioned is a sad and frustrating sight to behold. Either society "gets tough" and takes recourse to the most outdated and most obviously foolish defenses against shame, anxiety, and guilt, or it projects an aura of sentimentality and illusion, staring at the unfortunate chain of events which ended in a crime such as "this or that." It is generally only on two major issues that both extremes of society agree. First, that a solution to these problems must be given soon, and second, that such a solution must of course be simple and inexpensive.

Until perhaps just recently, even science was fooled by the old illusion that hatred, particularly of a youngster, is really only some sort of twisted love, and would quickly disappear by itself if someone could suggest ways of being nice to people

most if not all of the time. Accordingly, even professional literature has produced many more volumes on misguided and distorted love than volumes which deal directly with the phenomenon
of hatred.

When Freud disclosed his speculations on the severity of the
"death instinct" and the genuineness of some aggression and
destruction, many began to shudder enough to produce some
careful manifestations of aggression, at least as far as they
occurred with those of disorganized love or the fixated libido.

The various studies in *Frustration and Aggression* docu-
mented Freud's suspicions along that line cited above and have
shown statistically that the mere frustration of basic needs or
important goals in a child's life may be enough to produce
unmanageable quantities of aggression and destructiveness or
other disturbances even in children who otherwise would not
have had to hate so much.[103]

Many anthropologists have hinted with great enthusiasm at
the degree to which social customs and cultural mores can
increase or decrease the sum total of aggression engendered in
the members of a society, and have at times joined with
psychiatry in its speculations about the significant correlation
between adult aggression and the styles of early child care. One
thing is rather important to keep in mind, and that is that there
is still a wide gap between the hatred that a properly raised
middle-class child develops as a sideline to his anxiety or so-
called compulsion neurosis, and that of the slum area delinquent
who has to survive through the use of aggression in a "world
of struggle." There is a great difference between a child whose
basic personality is still in good enough condition to be approached through traditional psychological or psychiatric inter-
vention or through the design of a benevolent institutional
program, and a child in whom some of the most crucial normal
behavior controls have already been destroyed by those who
hated, abused, and neglected him so much when he was
dependent and weak—a child who by now is but a helpless,
resentful, frustrated, confused, fearful, distrustful, alienated bun-
dle of aggressive drives.

One of the major reasons behind the professional's inability to learn as much about this more extreme, more primitive, and more encompassing type of hatred and aggression as he has about, for example, the more neurosis-bound or more ego-controlled related but milder forms, is that children who hate very soon become the children nobody wants;[104] and by and large, neither the homes that originally produced them, nor the schools to which they go, nor the neighborhoods in which they play, nor the communities in which they live are willing or often able to cope with whatever behavior they project.

There are several signs and reasons for which these children become so ungovernable and intolerable to their respective communities. In some cases the anger is expressed, and in other instances it lies dormant, covert, under a surface of compliance, which lasts, by the way, only as long as it is convenient for the children to have it last. Others show no actual destructive tendencies at all, and seem to live in a withdrawn, distant sphere with either no relationships or at best superficial ones. One thing is certain, though; sooner or later the hostility shows itself and the respective communities and families become frustrated attempting to deal with even beginning to solve the difficulty.

These unwanted children become the children who trust nobody, regardless. Following the panic, confusion, desperation, and frustration of the family, it is usually the teacher who tries his hand in the matter. He soon gives up because "nothing seems to work; and believe me, I've tried everything." The adult who approaches them with firmness or even a wisely designed system of punishment will only find them stiffening their resistance and using all the conveniences of their pathology to fight the war with severe, constant, everyday battles of mischief. The educator who falls for some of their appealing antics, or more specifically, their temporary display of dependency pleas, soon finds them exploiting him mercilessly only to discard him as a "sucker" who never really cared for them at all any way, when further exploitation no longer seems to yield any results. The group worker who tries to lure them into more organized activities or to expose them to the challenge of heavily competitive team play will observe them either retreating in defeatist disgust or becoming so overtly excited that an unbridled tantrum materializes—or perhaps a prolonged sulk makes way. Foster parents, of course, cannot be expected to deal with them; they could not, and with other children in the home should not have to, put up, in the long run, with the disorganized and potentially dangerous behavior which these youngsters are able to produce. Some of them are happy for a while until the new foster parent happens to interfere with part of their pathology. Then, under the impact of trauma or fright, the full strength of their aggression overrides them. Others become unmanageable or run away as soon as the foster parent begins to be really loving and accepting; they find it so hard to accept the affection they seem so desperately to need and want. They are, at this stage of the game, impossible to trust in a children's institution or home, large or small. The peculiar perversity of their hate pathology makes them react even to a good diet of educational handling, and their presence often really makes the survival of other children in the same group a risk. When exposed to large and restrictive institutions, the routine structure only seems to feed their persecutory interpretation of life, and their inability to be grateful toward the friendly adult, or to take punishment in their stride and to learn from it, soon makes them isolated, unwanted, and disliked by everybody—other children as well as adults. The sociological gap between their natural life-style and the atmosphere of a psychiatrist's office is unsurmountable, and they cannot relate to an adult with whom they have a relationship only to talk or play.

Obviously, the children nobody knows how to deal with get in everyone's way. They can clog up the machinery in even the best of detention homes, which are not designed for their permanent care, but on which they are usually "dumped" after and between frantic attempts to palm them off on a farm, foster home, or an institution which has not yet caught on to them. Presently, some communities simply get angry at these children, exclude them from the school system, and "close the case after discussing it with a supervisor."

Of major importance here is for each of us to realize that although treatment of the children who hate is of utmost significance, it only takes second place to the problem of control with respect to "normal" children—a type of prevention rather than cure. However, with respect to the so-called ungovernable children, the reason why no one is able to reach them is simply because most of us get caught up in dealing with the hatred and aggression rather than the "decomposition of behavioral controls." Most fail to see how solidified their aggression is, and how it is so shrewdly organized to defend itself against moral implication. Treatment of such a child calls for a shifting from the emphasis on finding out what makes him tick to the question of studying the disturbances of his behavioral control function in greater detail, and with extreme consistency and organization. Regardless of how professionally most psychologists, psychiatrists, and social workers see themselves, it is this author's opinion that everyone still leaves basically most questions of punishment or reward, interference or permission, encouragement or criticism, approval or blame, etc., to trial and error, the convenience of the moment, or to popularized customs of our own childhood experiences, or to stereotyped philosophical beliefs.

Fritz Redl and David Wineman, in *The Aggressive Child*, tell us that there are three basic things about aggressive children which must be known before they can be worked with meaningfully: (1) what they are really like and why they do the things they do; (2) how people can work with and still survive with such children; and (3) what is the functional treatment necessary for these children?[105]

Before any of the above categories can be known, it must be realized that the most important single factor regarding such knowledge and technique involves living with the children, spending time with them, not only for the crisis situations, but also, and equally important, for the everyday, seemingly menial tasks. There must exist trained personnel who understand professionally, not so much emotionally, what were the catalysts within the child's background makeup.

Again, Fritz Redl and David Wineman state in their book that from their professional experiences and research they discovered that

> broken homes through divorce and desertion, the chain-reaction style of foster home placements and institutional storage, were conspicuous events in their lives. Aside from continuity, the quality of the tie between child and adult world was marred by rejection ranging from open brutality, cruelty and neglect, to affect barrenness on the part of some parents and narcissistic absorption in their own interests which exiled the child emotionally from them. . . . In this connection we were impressed by how little interest the parents took in what was happening to the children in treatment. Contrary to our expectations that they might become competitive with the treatment milieu on the basis of feelings of guilt for placing the child and for their own inadequacy, they never became involved on any level at all. Their main, unconcealed reaction was: "We're glad you've got them, not us. Life is so peaceful without them."
>
> This phenomenon of casual surrender of their own children marks these parents off decisively from the parents of the typical neurotic child who has had to go into institutional placement. The parents of the neurotic child who cannot live with the child also begin to feel in his absence that they cannot live without him either. He is somehow necessary to their neurotic design. This difference in the parental style of involvement with one's own child between the two groups is of very basic etiological significance in determining their contrasting symptom structures, since it is really the difference between little or no relationship at all, as we saw in our group, and an ambivalent but strong love-hate-ridden relationship.[106]

The whole vacuum in adult relationship potentialities cannot possibly be overestimated in terms of how impoverished these children feel or how much hatred and suspicion they have toward the entire adult world, particularly those representing control and authority.

Aggressive children in general have had very little in their lives which might be called either happy, good, or lucky. They

have not experienced being loved and wanted, or encouragement
and help to understand and accept basic values and standards
of the adult world around them; nor have they experienced
opportunities for and help in achieving a gratifying recreational
pattern, opportunities for adequate peer relationships, opportunities for formulating community ties, or adequate financial
security for some of their basic needs of life. Their energy to
get what they need and want as soon as possible and in any
way possible stems from the fact that their gratification of
needs was over-delayed.

It is important to realize that the aforementioned items were
missing from their environment, not that their behavior pre-
vented them from absorbing and utilizing them:

> If we tried to point out "future consequences" of anything they
> were about to do, we might as well have saved our breath. For
> what is trouble which might be brewing for tomorrow, no matter
> how fatal, compared with even mild fun right now? . . . What
> "ego ideals" they were swaggering around with, if existent at
> all, were totally delusionary and mostly borrowed from radio,
> movie or comic book, and even then only on a flighty "enjoyment
> of present illusions" basis.[107]

In other words, in brief, some of these children's so-called social
blindness failures were simply a result of fixation on the basis of
neglect. This part of their thought processes and behavior patterns can usually by corrected simply by education; by exposure
to interpreted, felt, explained, interrupted experience; by the
ability to make use of valid inferences from previous experiences.
And that is the worst of it regarding severely aggressive youngsters—for if the ability to draw realistic inferences from what
happens to others is seriously impaired, not only will such
children not learn from what they hear about life and what
they see happen to others, but it is even difficult to make use
of such incidents to argue with their own "more terrible" self;
and it is logical argument by a well-related person which usually
is the single most important factor in ego-supportive therapy.

There should be little wonder, then, that children as disjointed as those being discussed in this paper have special problems when confronted with success and failure, or even when confronted with the simple admission of a mistake. Many of these youngsters are so fatalistically afraid and convinced of the unavoidability of failure that they withdraw from some fields entirely, or develop tremendous resistance against even trying under the most favorable conditions. For them, the admission of an insignificant mistake in turn is usually met by one of two reactions—either it is considered just more evidence that "I'm no good at that anyway, so what's the use of trying?" or the person who administers criticism immediately is pushed into the role of a hostile, mutilating, unappreciative adult. But even the overlooking or ignoring of mistakes later recognized as such by the child backfires more often than not. It is turned into its opposite, and interpreted as lack of interest in the child's progress, lack of helpfulness, or sheer stupidity on the adult's part.

The legal concept of delinquency simply states which type of behavior is forbidden by law, in which state, for which age group of children, etc. This is all it can do. It is obviously no help at all for whomever wants to know just what a piece of behavior means, how it was caused, or what should be done to avoid or cure it. It is worthwhile, though, to know about legal definitions so that one can assess the reality impact of certain issues in a number of cases.

The cultural meaning of the word delinquency might summarize all statements indicating that a piece of behavior is in contradiction with the value demands of the dominant culture within which a given child moves. Of course, there is no rigid system of values which would be valid for everybody in any one given culture, and so it must be constantly kept in mind that such a definition has many faults and limitations.

The clinical concept of delinquency is not in contradiction with the cultural or legal ones, but should be considered as an attempt to specify and supplement where the others left off.

The term "delinquent-ego" as used by Redl and Wineman is significant here. They use the term with two things in mind.

First, the term refers to any behavior that runs counter to the dominant value system within which the child's character formation takes place. "Thus we would include his insistence on 'hate without cause,' even where no clearly legally punishable act was involved. We mean all the attitudes which will be developed in a child who is about to drift into a 'delinquent style of life'." Second, the term describes the ego in those situations in which it is bent on "defending impulse gratification at any cost. In short, instead of performing its task of looking for a synthesis between desires, reality demands and the impact of social values, the ego is, in those moments, totally on the side of impulsivity."[108]

This ego type delinquent is very different from the delinquent who is loaded with alibis, tricks, deceptions, etc. He has masterminded a "system of delusions" in order to talk himself out of the demands of his own conscience, where it is still intact; i.e.: (1) "He did it first," (2) "Everybody does it," (3) "We were all in on it," (4) "It was done to me several times," (5) "He deserved it," (6) "I had to do it or lose my dignity," (7) "I really didn't get a big charge out of it anyway," (8) "I can always make up with him," (9) "He's no good anyway," (10) "Everybody is always picking on me," (11) "I couldn't have gotten it any other way."[109]

Now, although the alibiing delinquent uses most, if not all, of the above system, as does the ego-delinquent, it is most important to realize that an efficient delinquent ego is not satisfied with inventing just alibis and schemes to put its conscience to rest. It reaches out more actively for opportunities circumscribing the guiltless enjoyment of delinquent gratifications, such as: (1) ferreting out the "wrong" type of friends, (2) moving toward gang formation and mob psychology, (3) provoking the initiatory act (considering themselves from any cognitive dissonance or value conflicts; e.g., when the delinquent-ego provokes another and that person responds, the response is seen as the initial provocation), (4) hankering toward delinquent lure (i.e., placing oneself in situations that will tempt one's impulsivity), (5) exploiting moods (e.g., staging a tantrum so that it takes precedence over the original question of the adult, such as "Why did you not go to school today?"), (6) rebelling for someone else's cause, (7) cultivating delinquency-prone ego ideals (i.e., denying the desire for delinquent exploits, and identifying with an ego-ideal of a person whose image is secondarily encouraging delinquent fun), (8) imagining exceptional exemption from the laws of cause and effect (i.e., I have luck, skill, wisdom, power, etc.; with power, luck, etc., on one's side, fear as well as guilt become unnecessary); and (9) depending on delinquency-tied ambitions and skills (i.e., "This is the only  profession I know and can make a living at in your society, and it's too late for me to change.").[110]

There is no greater threat to a delinquent-ego as that which attempts to procure change. Six major techniques are generally employed by the ego in its defense against change: (1) confessional constipation (the delinquent clams up entirely), (2) escape to virtue (when pressure is really applied, the delinquent will produce some of the changes the adults seem to be keen on, without any real commitment or surrender, (3) group ostracism against those who reform, (4) avoidance of delinquency-dangerous personnel (e.g., people too friendly, funny, affectionate, nice, etc.), (5) refusal to give up delinquency-prone life factors (the delinquent who seems to function best where life is rough on him, and who seems to run away or become hopelessly restless when he really "gets a break."), (6) strangulation of love, dependency, and activity requirements (i.e., "the safest way to not get involved and remain 'free' from disappointment, unhappiness, or discomfort is to stop wanting anything.").[111]

There is even a deeper stage of the delinquent-ego which involves the most vigilant of these so committedly angry youngsters, and that is where the delinquent cannot be satisfied with defending himself against the temptation toward change. Over and beyond this, he will be confronted with situations where change agents are thrown into his life in the form of educators and clinicians who make a frontal attack on his position. In those instances he has to be ready, and is, to deal directly with any personal effort at change. A good delinquent-ego usually has a whole "mechanized" arsenal of direct defense techniques at its disposal, the seven primary ones being: (1) diagnostic acuity in battle-relevant areas (all of a sudden the otherwise cognitively deficient egos develop hypertrophic skills, such as extreme perception in a conversation, and the like), (2) the legalistic mind (any time these youngsters catch an adult in an inconsistency, or a premature bluff or attempt to call their bluff before it could be proven, or an insinuation of a motive for which insufficient evidence was obvious, etc., they react as though this proved the adults were wrong all the time), (3) expertise in the manipulation of people and chance, (4) absurdity of demand (i.e., something unattainable at the moment is demanded immediately. When it is not gotten, the adults are seen as selfish, hostile, and unloving, (5) anticipatory provocation (the delinquent tries to produce at all expense anger, fury, wrath, attack, and even punishment from the adult so that these reactions can be scrutinized at opportune moments), (6) organized defamation (an organized campaign of gossip propaganda that purposely misinterprets the motives of what the adult is really trying to do), and (7) friendship without influence (playing on the adult's personal love demands and narcissism; e.g., being liked, preferred and popular with the kids is much more gratifying than an arduous and highly ambivalent relationship with them).[112]

In this chapter the primary discussion has involved the major difficulties to be faced by anyone attempting to work with aggressive youngsters. In the upcoming chapter attention is shifted to the question of suggested treatment for these children —techniques to help gain control from within the person rather than externally from either other persons or the environment at large.

Control and Reduction of Aggression

To understand the rationale behind the innumerous theories of causation regarding violence and, more specifically, violent crime, is one thing; but to intelligently deal with the dynamics involved with such concepts as the elimination, control, and/or reduction of aggression is by far something else.

Since this paper primarily deals with the concept of prevention more so than cure, it follows that this chapter should realistically discuss the necessary strategy circumscribing the decrease of violence as it relates to children rather than adults. And so, the following pages will be basically pertaining to youngsters between the ages of one through approximately sixteen. However, it must be kept in mind continuously that there is a great difference between knowing what to do in a situation on one hand, and knowing exactly how to do it on the other. Therefore, simply listing the things which must be done and things which must not be done to reduce violence in our society is in and of itself insufficient. There is an art involved on the implementation of the knowledge; hence, certain traits such as perception, intuition, timing, personal concern, empathy, awareness, and sensitivity all become extremely important when considering the actual mechanisms needed to produce an effective and positive therapeutic environment.

The scope of this thesis does not include the above-mentioned "magical touch" that some people undoubtedly have. Such a consideration would obviously take additional as well as different research than that used in this thesis, and would necessarily have to be viewed in a more philosophical than scientific manner. It, this thesis that is, will include, however, suggestions as to what might initiate a program which purports to reduce violence, which unlike so many, will encompass more than just professional custodial care.

First of all, to defensive, angry, insecure, and distrustful children, the immediate atmosphere or environment is of extreme importance. Without the proper foundation, no program is able to function at maximum capacity; and so, such base things as the location of say, for example, a therapeutic Group Home, the architectural design, the space, distribution of the home, the color combinations inside the building, the arrangement and type of furnishings, the equipment, and even the style of housekeeping become of paramount importance. Once the setting is established and maintained, once the materialistic sectors are taken care of, then the program can proceed to its next and comparatively more important stages.

No attempt should be made to duplicate or imitate the natural habitat of the child. To create a slum or ghetto environment so that a youngster from a slum area will feel at home is absurd. On the other hand, however, it is essential to avoid too great extremes, causing the youngster to panic due to the newness of the situation. It would not then generally be advantageous to place a ghetto youth into a community where the average family income is $100,000 a year.

Once a child is in treatment residency, a margin of destructiveness and misuse must be anticipated by the entire staff. Chairs, for instance, are meant to be sat on. However, standing on them at times by youngsters who are anxiously involved in some type of game may have to be overlooked from time to time. This does not mean that the children should be allowed to do anything they want. It does mean, though, that under some circumstances they should be permitted to trespass somewhat the fringe of normal use. At its extreme, at times a "real" treatment home will have to expect and accept a margin of destruction and waste.

In working with ego-disturbed children, however, it is important to stress the danger of going too far with regard to leniency or super-permissiveness. The kind of children being discussed here have very low temptation resistance and few controls, and even those are easily dissipated during moments of excitement caused from overstimulation. For their ego to keep some level of reasonable control, therefore, it is also important that open overstimulation or overseductiveness of surroundings and props is carefully avoided.

Children should pick up on the whole style of housekeeping and the basic policies expressed in the way the house is run. These trends, of course, have an effect on them. The youngsters quickly realize whether the adults of the home emphasize an "enjoy yourself," "lived-in" quality, or if they instead are more concerned with the protection of the value of the possessions themselves. Since youngsters would react negatively in most cases to either extreme, not only as a part of a realistic regime, but also as a part of a psychological gesture of the relationship of adults to them, such considerations must be made an important item in staff selection and training. This selection and training must include "all" of the staff. "The people who often have to bring the greatest personal and professional sacrifices to the principle of clinical hygiene are the janitor and the cook."[113]

Many lay and professional people have a distorted idea of the concept of "routine." Either they feel that without a schedule which designates what should be done at every moment the program will collapse, or they envision routine as a boxing-in phenomenon, which leaves no space for creativity or originality.

The professional should, of course, take it for granted that the phenomenon of routine is a complex one. The true professional, then, sees routine as neither good nor bad, and his personal attitudes concerning routine definitely are not chosen as the yardstick for his value for a specific child or group of children. Rather, "objective criteria must be found on the basis of which we can make decisions as to where in the life of a group of children routines are needed and what kind of routine would be most available."[114] For example, an institution maintaining ten thousand youngsers would by necessity require more routine implantation than a Group Home with a residency of eight.

Routine must have periodic insertions of ego-supportive values, even though such diversions may interfere with the managerial smoothness of the operation from time to time. Specific content of expediency routines must have ingenuity and design, even when, for example, it appears as though all ingenious ideas have been tried and proven fruitless.

Obviously, awakening most children, problemed or not, and getting them washed, clothed, fed, and off to school on time involves a certain amount of routinization, particularly since the time available for such tasks is most assuredly finite. Now, from an administrative expediency point of view, solutions to such problems appear very simple, solutions such as: (a) using a louder bell or alarm system to awake the youngsters, (b) getting the staff to move faster and more efficiently, (c) putting the children to bed earlier, (d) punishing the children if they do not get to school on time, and (e) holding meetings explaining to the youngsters that a certain problem can no longer be tolerated, etc. Enacting any or all of the above "may" save time, staff, and personnel, and just "may" get the children to school on time; but, however, study after study after study seems to support the fact that the children

go off to school with such an amount of mutual hostility, of anxiety or aggressive pressure, of inner group conflict or of destroyed morale in terms of the subsequent school job that the next person who received them from us could not possibly have done anything worthwhile with them. To plan for an appropriate routine for the morning hour, therefore, it became necessary and important to consider the type of procedure which would cope with the emotional problem of the situation most adequately. During the phase of our treatment . . . we devised the following process, which at the time proved to be the most salutary way out all around: "The counselor would turn up about ten minutes before waking was even necessary, putter around in the playroom and in the children's bedroom, sort out clothes and perform all sorts of tasks, as might a mother in a home who is up before the children are ready for breakfast. Those children who would not gradually wake up in the process would do so when the counselor turned on the radio with a soft volume. The children who were awakened would be approached in a friendly way by the adult and they would be reassured that it was not time to get up yet, that they could still keep their eyes closed and stay in bed for a while, and that the counselor would come back and tell them when it really was time. At the time when getting up became essential, some of the youngsters were ready for the process without as much hostility as they usually show in their transaction from their sleep and dream world to reality."[115]

And so, in many institutional settings it is not so much the routine itself and its planning which cause friction, but the over-excited manner in which either the children or the adults react to the item of routine.

Any treatment program must satisfy the youngsters. If the children are unhappy, then the program is failing, regardless of how it looks on paper. Many treatment homes have their main ambition focused on the existence of sufficient psychiatric, psychological, and social work consultation, adequate and increased casework staff, and the selection of personnel who are nonpunitive and accept the children who are to be treated. Although all of the above qualities are without a doubt most important in a therapeutic atmosphere, all-too-often, however, program planning and its details are entirely neglected in such clinical plans. The primary belief seems to be that, if children are given love, affection, time, understanding, and enough interviews, they will respond positively, change their lives, and become loving and giving human beings for life; that if the children are busy, communicative and nondestructive, everything is going well.

The above ideas are based unfortunately on a misunderstanding of the basic role of the program and of the psychiatric nature of the impact of activity on the total economy of a child's impulse-control balance.

Children often appraise the amount of affection or rejection which they receive from adults primarily through activity channels. Besides, the unavoidable frequency of interference by adults or of situations which to the children are frustrating cuts down the amount of direct love signals which the adults can give. The most friendly and affectionate adult is perceived by them in many moments of the day as a hostile, negative inteferer and even as an enemy. A treatment home, therefore, especially in the beginning, has to rely heavily on indirect channels of communication of acceptedness and affection from adults. One of the safest channels of that sort is the amount of gratification the children receive during a day and the willingness and enjoyment on the side of the adult with whom they are allowed to receive it. In fact, children may engage in the happiest recreational enterprises, but, if they think that the adults frown upon them, they then interpret these enterprises not as a symbol of love from adults, but as a triumphant prize won against their vigilance. It is therefore important that the institution as a whole and every person in it are openly and explicitly acceptant of children having fun. This means that even where fun-bringing activities have to be interfered with, it is the "reality limitations" attitude that has to be conveyed. Hostility toward fun itself must not be displayed by the adult.[116]

Besides wanting an adult to be concerned, loving, understanding, friendly, and affectionate, children, especially those with ego disturbances, silently demand that the adult serve as their protector. To name just a few anxiety-provoking situations, these children, from time to time, fear: (1) loss of their self-control, (2) other children's actions and threats, (3) parents' turning up unexpectedly to punish or take them away, (4) the police arresting them for some misdeed of the past, (5) some dangerous person from their previous lives suddenly appearing on the scene, and (6) extreme and confusing situations—to name but a few.

Delinquent children must be able to produce a good deal of behavior which is natural to their disturbance, even though it may be risky, undesirable, and in conflict. This entails a tremendous degree of patience on the part of all staff members, since it encompasses a great deal of what will be called here "system tolerance." In other words, much behavior—for example, smirks, wise comments, and the like, which should not be accepted from the ego-balanced individual—might well have to be almost totally ignored as it is projected by the ego-disturbed individual.

"In order for ego-disturbed children even to begin to function adequately, it is essential that they get a heavy dose of affection, as well as gratifying life experiences. They need those doses as the basis on which treatment can even be considered, not as the removable reward for good behavior."[117]

Regardless of how well any individual is responding to any treatment milieu, periods of regression and escapism are to date inevitable. Even the most perfectly designed of all programs would not be abe to account for all the needs of all the youngsters at any one particular point in time. Therefore, any residential home must make it possible to build phases of nearly total regression to earlier childhood developments and infantile need demands in the total style and to still be able to manipulate the more realistic level of operation of a total group at the same time.

> An experience may be traumatic for an organism on two counts. Either it hits too close to home in terms of experiences which have happened to that organism before and have produced a disturbance in it, or it is so wrongly constructed by its very nature that the organism afflicted by it could not be expected to stand up under its impact. In short, you can produce a traumatic effect either by mild pressure on an already inflamed corn or by dropping a fifty-pound weight on a healthy toe. Whether an experience will have a traumatic effect or not, and which experience will, depends, therefore, to a high degree on (a) the previous traumatizations which have taken place in the earlier history of the children and their specific nature, and (b) the structure of the life situations to which they are exposed and their impact on the specific developmental stage of the child.[118]

Total protection from traumatic life situations is neither achievable nor desirable. Life does contain painful occurrences which everyone must eventually learn to face. Nevertheless, any institution must avoid any type of exposure to traumatization situations in its own programming, handling, and design. And so, total avoidance of unhealthy handling of the youngsters by the institutional staff must be a necessity, not a goal:

> Under no circumstances can a person in an institution afford techniques of handling children which by their very nature establish a traumatic risk. Thus, any form of physical punishment whatsoever is totally excluded, the use of threat or promise in order to handle the momentary comfort of the adult is out, the absolute avoidance of exposure of the children to threat and fear, on the one hand, and over-competitive challenge on the other, must be enforced. . . . Over and above this guarantee from traumatic handling, it is important to remain sensitive to the previous traumatization history of a child.[119]

Programming of a treatment home must, of course, be organized, but that fact in no way insinuates that it cannot be flexible; and it must. For example, group units, as well as being kept small, must remain malleable. Sometimes, as a result of confusion, overstimulation, or anxiety-producing occurrences, re-grouping is necessary so that during these periods the individual is kept free from other pressures.

Intake and exclusion policies regarding referrals must be clinically defined. "It is impossible to keep the atmosphere of a treatment home intact if outside pressures like Board or community feelings have the chance to destroy a consistent atmosphere whenever they feel like it. The staff of a treatment home must be able to decide the intake or exclusion of a child on entirely clinical and group psychological criteria with no other strings attached."[120]

For clinical reasons, at times an immediate program change is necessary. This means that the institution must be equipped with enough personnel to split groups in half or quarters when needed, to switch from indoor to outdoor activities, to change from a much-anticipated planned trip outside to a stay-at-home activity, etc. In brief, there must be sufficiently adequate personnel and equipment for all types of emergency assistance.

A good deal of child behavior carries within its own limited intensity charge, which lessens by itself automatically as soon as the intensity is exhausted. The skill of selection of which behavior the adult should interfere with, and which behavior he should ignore, is very important to the child's behavior patterns. All professionals should be aware of the fact that, many times, ignoring certain behavior makes it easier for the child to stop that behavior.

Every worthwhile teacher and counselor knows how stages of excitement, anxiety, and restlessness are occasionally simply depleted by increasing the physical proximity between child and adult. However, since with some youngsters proximity is insufficient, some type of direct physical contact seems to be required at times. Knowing when to touch—e.g., patting on the back, placing one's hand on the child's shoulder, touching the hand, etc.—is an art in itself, and is an enterprise which all persons dealing with disturbed youngsters should possess.

It is also of great importance that the adult who is dealing with youngsters should have a high involvement-interest relationship with the children to whom he is assigned. Although most youngsters desire to have adults take an interest in their interests, with disturbed children such a need is more emphatic and usually continues far beyond the years of early childhood. The child who gets bored or disinterested or anxious about a task he is doing poorly oftentimes will become rejuvenated when an adult he is fond of simply asks him a few questions about what he is doing or gives him a chance to explain.

Sometimes all that is needed for a child's ego or superego to regain control in the face of anxiety or impulsivity is a sudden additional quantity of affection, the lack of which seems to be disastrous. The willingness to give and express such affection on the part of the adult at any given time is essential to the child's trust and understanding of the involved adult. Children with ego disturbances may have trouble accepting the more traditional forms of affection, or even admitting their need for them. However, the unconscious need pattern frequently is still in a very similar stage to that of the much younger child.

After a certain amount of ego improvement, even the most

severe and obviously pathological temper tantrums of a specific child can suddenly be avoided with a well-timed injection of humor:

> Speculation about the basic machinery involved here may differ on the basic theoretical framework from which the problem is tackled, and is still a puzzle to us. A hunch is that we probably deal with a combination of several factors: (a) we demonstrate the invulnerability of the adult; (b) the child, through the humor response, is saved from extra guilt feelings or fear by which he was just about to be overcome in the process of attack or the production of problem behavior; (c) the possibility of face-saving is extended especially in cases where youngsters work themselves up into a demonstration of attack or toughness over and beyond what they are quite ready to live up to, so that the offering of a humorous means of avoiding these implications is experienced as a great relief; (d) in some cases a humorous reaction may actually make it possible for a youngster to get such intensive satisfaction out of the "funniness" or "wittiness" of the moment that this overbalances whatever other emotional processes are keeping him tied up at the time.[121]

Obviously there are more complicated factors involved in this mechanism. However, the above factors are sufficient to cover the scope and range of the subject intended by this paper.

Helping the youngsters to understand the meaning of a situation which they have misinterpreted, or to help them grasp their own motivations during issues at hand, takes great patience and is essential to the organization of the child's thought processes. With reality placed back into its rightful position, the child's negative behavior oftentimes becomes unnecessary to him and as a result may be discontinued.

One of the most frequent mistakes of the unskilled educator is that of thinking that he always has to interfere with the youngster's antisocial behavior by drastic means, when a simple appeal directly to the youngster would suffice:

> It is important to gauge the area in which a youngster may be potentially ready to allow an approach by direct appeal to work, the conditions under which such an appeal or approach is at all

possible, and the major reality issues involved in the timing and selection of this in contrast to other situations where more direct action is indicated. On the other hand, it is, of course, clinically valuable, provided an equal action effect can be obtained, that even simple realistic needs for interference be met by direct appeal, if that is possible, rather than by other more frustration-and-battle-producing interference techniques. The most frequently used basis for appeal which adults employ in the daily battle with child behavior can be listed as follows: (a) appeal to personal relationship ("Please don't do this. I don't think this is fair to me."), (b) physical reality implication ("Say, you can't do this. It's dangerous, you know."), (c) undesirable consequences inherent in the act ("Listen, if you saw the wood recklessly, you'll break it and then your gun won't hold."), (d) outside role sensitivities ("Say, we can't get away with that. You know that people won't at all stand for this behavior in the bowling alleys."), (e) superego demand and value sensitivity ("Come on, you don't want to be like that!"), (f) group code value ("I don't think the kids would think that's fair."), (g) narcissistic pride ("Oh come, you don't want to run around like that with all the other people looking at us."), (h) appraisal of community consequences ("Listen, if you get caught for this, you know what will happen."), (i) awareness of peer group reaction ("You can't expect the other kids to like you if you continue messing up their fun."), (j) hierarchical limitation awareness ("Well, I guess I can't stop you, but you know that Fritz won't let you get away with this."), (k) personal considerations ("Please stop banging on the door. I really need my sleep right now. I've been up all night."), (l) pride in personal improvement ("Oh come on, you don't have to act that silly any more. You know better now.").[122]

When dealing with any individual's behavior, influence on that behavior is best obtained through mild reprimand for that which is done wrong, and strong, though not unrealistic or overly dramatic, approval of that which is done correctly. Most psychological research on behavior modification suggests that such is the most effective way to deal with behavior which is long-lasting and strongly habitual. However, surprisingly enough, for children who have somehow learned to hate, neither reward nor punishment is as strong of a deterrent as most might expect. Among those factors which do not allow promises and rewards to be as influential as they might be under normal circumstances are: (1) the inability of an ego-disturbed child to feel that he deserves anything, (2) his inability to interpret the present in correct relationship to his own past or future, (3) his inability to accept a reward without simultaneously comparing it to either what some other child is receiving or has received, (4) the child's fatalistic concept of life, and (5) his inability to see a reward as anything without strings attached to it.

In contrast to promises and rewards are the mechanisms behind threats and punishment, per se. Although neither psychiatry nor psychology has as yet contributed definitively with regard to the actual effect of punishment—and although such psychological and sociological research tends to suggest that punishment has more negative than positive effects on human behavior—there are, however, conditions which must be existent before such a control method can be effective:

(a) The punishment situation must be experienced as something unpleasant. (b) Frustration or aggression produced by such an experience of "pain" must be related to the real issue at stake and not confused with the person who inflicted it. (c) The aggression inflicted and generated through punishment-inflicted pain or unpleasantness must be internalized and directed toward that part of the personality which produced the problem to begin with. (d) The aggression produced through punishment must be internalized in such a way that it will effectively control the impulses in question rather than produce defense, anxiety, aggressive stages, or self-recrimination and withdrawal.[123]

It is of vital importance that the child being punished understands both that it is his behavior that has been disapproved of and not himself as a person, and that it is his behavior that has brought on the punishment and not the adult who happens to have been assigned to carry it out. Needless to say, any punishment must be carried out as soon after the disapproved behavior as possible.

In order to reduce and control violence and crime, in addition to working with individuals and their personal difficulties, it is of paramount importance and significance to also be involved with the innumerable political and sociological factors which without question play an important role in the increase or decrease of aggressive behavior. To begin with, more time and energy must be given to such things as architectural layout of buildings, location and grouping of such buildings, and the lighting of these buildings, within the framework of a particular community.

People within a community must be encouraged to know one another better and more meaningfully. It is this knowledge which reduces fear between people, and the confusion and criticism with regard to the behavior of others; in brief, this knowledge reduces prejudices.

Although it has been argued by some that when guns are outlawed only outlaws will have guns, statistics suggest repeatedly that murderers, for example, are relatively average people with no long history of previous violence, and that it more often than not is the availability of a weapon during an emotional outburst that makes them murderers instead of assaulters.

There are several actions still considered by legal authorities to be of a criminal nature that in actuality should not be considered criminal at all. In other words, one way to reduce crime is by reducing crimes, such as victimless ones. Persons with drug addiction difficulties should be considered persons with psychological problems rather than with criminal or legal problems, and thus should be also considered in need of help rather than punishment.

The President's Commission on Law Enforcement and Administration of Justice had a number of suggestions for improving police effectiveness and impartiality, some of which are consistent with the psychological principles and research cited in this book. Included among their thirty-five recommendations are the following: (a) Establish community relations units in departments serving substantial minority population. (b) Establish citizeny advisory committees in minority-group neighborhoods. (c) Recruit more minority-group officers. (d) Emphasize community relations in training and operations. (e) Provide adequate procedures for processing citizen grievances against all public officials. (f) Recruit more actively, especially maximums, to competitive levels. (g) Set as goal, requirement of baccalaureate degree for general enforcement officers. (h) Stress ability in promotion. (i) Develop and enunciate policy guidelines for exercise of law enforcement discretion. (j) Establish strong internal investigation units in all departments to maintain police integrity. (k) Experiment with team policing combining patrol and investigative units. (l) Adopt policy limiting use of firearms by officers.[124]

Nearly forty specific recommendations for changes in the operations of the court system were made by the President's Commission of Law Enforcement and Administration of Justice; and a number of others have called for a variety of changes in the structure and operation of the courts: (a) Increase judicial manpower. (b) Enact comprehensive state bail reform legislation. (c) Establish state house release and summons procedure. (d) Revise sentencing provisions of penal codes. (e) Establish probation services in all courts for presentence investigation of every offender. (f) Institute procedures for promoting just and uniform sentencing. (g) Institute timetable for completion of criminal cases.

Two additional changes can be recommended: elimination of the intermediate sentence and elimination of secretive plea-bargaining. [125]

While prison reform has repeatedly been demanded over the past hundred years or so, no successful efforts to deal humanely with convicts have ever been instituted on a wide scale. That such a concept is feasible

. . . can be seen from the fact that even prison administrators agree that between seventy-five and ninety percent of all prisoners would, if freed immediately, present no danger or threat to the community. This is consistent with the literature showing that most crimes, including personal crimes, are committed by relatively average people in rather atypical situations rather than being committed by atypical persons in normal situations.[126]

Particularly important for a reduction in the future occurrence of criminal aggression is the provision of juveniles who have already shown signs of criminality or excessive violence with alternative behavior. The types of training which may be expected to reduce antisocial behavior include increasing the individual's ability to foresee the consequences of his or her actions and increasing the ability to verbalize rather than act out his or her feelings.

A study by Alexander and Parsons involved the fostering of communication and negotiation skills among members of delinquents' families. Recidivism rates for delinquents in these experimental families were compared with those delinquents receiving client-centered family therapy, church-sponsored family counseling, or no treatment. The results of the study showed that the lowest recidivism rate (26%) was for those delinquents who, along with their families, received instruction in communicating and negotiating, while the highest recidivism rate (73%) was for those receiving family counseling. The recidivism rates for the client-centered groups (47%) and the no treatment groups (50%) were about the same as the recidivism rate for the country as a whole (51%).[127]

There are a number of ways in which the reward structure in relation to violence can be altered. One is to increase the personal costs of violent behavior, primarily through the public condemnation of violence; another is to decrease the positive reinforcements for engaging in violence; and a third is to provide alternative ways of arriving at desirable goals without the need to resort to violence.

Although much criticism has been directed by many toward the mass media and its influence on human behavior, it seems more practical that emphasis should be placed on teaching individuals to behave and think rationally, and with purpose, rather than impulsively as a result of what they believe the majority of others are doing.

According to Arnold Arnold, author of *Violence and Your Child*, there are sixteen basic ways to reduce violence in your child:

1. Be loving to your child.
2. Reward and discipline your child realistically.
3. Teach your child verbal violence and threats, as much as physical aggression, must be considered in the light of a scale of alternatives.

4. Encourage your child to non-violently defend and understand himself and his views.
5. Set examples to your child which are fair and non-violent in your dealings with him and with all others, in and outside of your family.
6. Set worthwhile goals for your child and encourage him to discover things on his own.
7. Give your child historic insights by telling him stories of your childhood and about major events in which you participated nonaggressively.
8. Make light of commercial pressures on your child and expose promotional deceptions or seduction for whatever they are.
9. Do not allow your child daily and for long periods of time unsupervised television viewing until he is at least ten or twelve years old.
10. Discuss the implications and consequences of television shows, comics, movies, etc.
11. Ban all violent comic books and sadistic magazines from your home unless you have the time and knowledge to explain and discuss their hidden implications and consequences.
12. Ban all toys of violence.
13. Tell your child stories and read to him as early as the age of one year old.
14. Familiarize yourself with the plots and contents of books and movies your child sees before you give or let him read or see them.
15. Let your child become aware that all parental restrictions will be lifted gradually as he becomes older and is better able to make his own value judgments.
16. In making value judgments about violent television shows, movies, etc., a parent must concern himself with the context in which violence is placed.[128]

In brief, to curtail crime in the immediate future to any significant extent, and to prevent its occurrence in the long run, it will be necessary to change our current ways of conceptualizing it and of dealing with it; it will be necessary for us to teach our youth to think things out in a rational way before acting.

Summary
and Conclusion

Studying and understanding the etiology of aggression is obviously a very complicated task. There is innumerable research material which lends support to almost any possible, conceivable theory, and the controversy between and among the theories and the research behind them will more likely than not continue to exist for many years to come. However, this thesis has supported more so those views and concepts which see aggression and, more specifically, criminal violence, as the by-product of the illogical, ambivalent, and contradictory values, systems, and norms within society. This outlook in no way insinuates that the individual is not basically responsible for his behavior, especially since psychological factors are heavily concentrated throughout any political or sociological dilemmas which may exist at any particular time or place; persons have to be disorganized before societies can be disorganized. What this point of view does support, however, is that it is extremely difficult for "persons" to persist with rational, altruistic, and meaningful behavior, when "people" as a whole function illogically, fearfully, imitatively, and meaninglessly, often looking to the next person before determining what they should think or do with regard to their own needs, desires, and fantasies.

In discussing criminal aggression, this thesis has attempted to show that although there may be physiological factors, for example, involved with some aggressive behavior, the major cause-effect routine is most often initiated through the learning process; unfortunately, most of us learn "what" to think and feel, instead of "how" to think and feel. Since learning seems to be most impressive—that is in so far as formulating and organizing thought and behavior patterns during the earlier stages of one's life—it seems to follow that handling conflicts at an early age is more likely to prevent future more serious ones than to undo hurt and damage inflicted over a period of many years.

The idea of instinctive aggression has not been supported by this paper, and, so, neither has been the belief that man must learn to accept his natural aggressive composition. Several ways have been suggested concerning how one might begin dealing with the complexities of crime and aggression, and it has been simultaneously insinuated that people will respond more reasonably when the more responsible sector of society's population teaches them to think and act originally, selflessly, rationally, and constructively, rather than imitatively, impulsively, fearfully, and thoughtlessly.

If society is going to implant values, dreams, desires, and success as goals worthy of attainment through delay of gratification, then, most assuredly it is going to have to concurrently implant the means by which they can be obtained.

> We must begin to modify our adult society, the real adult society in which our children are being raised, if we are to reduce aggression. We must work toward a level of morality more civilized than the "lex talionis" of an eye for an eye, and a tooth for a tooth. We must provide for parents, school administrators and governmental authorities, alternatives to the current reliance on physical punishment and other aggression-provoking methods for discipline and behavioral control. We must train our children to relate to one another and especially to members of other ethnic and racial groups as individual human beings rather than as stereotypes. It is easy to commit acts of violence when the policeman is dehumanized into a "pig" and the student into a "hippie."[129]

Clearly, the public has not panicked over white-collar crime, nor crimes of passion, nor organized crime, nor political crimes. Indeed, these are important matters, but they are not really the force that is shaking the foundations of correction theory. It is violent street crimes which have everyone in fear of their lives, which have caused us to re-route some of our most vital daily routines, and which either prevent us from doing things we once did, or restricts them to such a degree that caution necessarily overrides enjoyment.

Although it is violent street crime which is the red menace of this generation, it is not believed by this writer that a man's soul can be therapeutically reformed by coercion. We need programs which provide relief from boredom and idleness, conditions which are certainly among the greatest causes of violence in our prisons as they are the causes of crime in our streets.

Many people strongly feel that prisons, for example, should be totally abolished on the grounds of their obvious failure to reform the multitude of offenders exposed to them. These people rest their case on studies showing that institutionalization frequently increases the probability of recidivism, just as it increases the anger and alienation of the inmate.

Some support for the abolitionists' position can be found in the successful closing of youth training schools in Massachusetts. Since 1970, that State has reduced the number of youths in secure facilities from 1,000 to 1,000 minus 900. In place of cells, the State now relies on foster homes, group homes, and a system of advocates to keep these offenders out of trouble. These advocates are not professional social workers, nor do they enforce laws or report violations. Their role is to help youths select living arrangements, find and keep jobs, choose educational programs, and to intercede with public officials on behalf of their charges. The theory is that kids will fight any program that is bureaucratic, repressive, and adversarial, but will respond when they are shown personal attention and real concern. At least the initial data seem to support this theory. Foster care and the advocate system are proving more effective in reducing recidivism rates than are Group Homes.[130]

If our goal is to reduce street violence, more is needed than simple deinstitutionalization or additional probation officers. Even one-on-one supervision will not suffice. We must look to the condition which bred the crime in the first place, or else expect the offender to again break the law when he is returned to those conditions.

Some offenders simply must be incarcerated to protect society; otherwise, we face the prospect of escalating street violence. Although many would certainly agree that this dangerous offender must be imprisoned, the problem remains with defining "dangerous" and then finding the tools to measure it.

"Where there is no alternative to incarceration, we should consider new approaches. The most basic change that can be made is to reduce the size of our prisons. Experience shows that our super fortresses housing thousands of inmates carry a built-in brutality. Control over these huge populations tends to come by harsh disciplinary measures, or not at all."[131]

Total uniformity of sentencing in this country would be disastrous. If we are to remain a democracy, we must insist on some forms of sentencing discretion. To do away with individualized justice would be an insult to our constitution. Surely review procedures by panels of judges at the trial or appellate level can end wide disparities in sentencing without ignoring differences in offenders which justify different treatment and consideration. Shifting from concern for the individual to mathematical or mechanical principles of fairness may well have us eventually forgetting the individual altogether.

Unfortunately, much controversy exists between and among agencies within the criminal justice system. "The whole system of corrections, from sentencing to parole, being so largely empty of communicable rationalities, is shrouded in silence and filled with barriers between those who should be talking and collaborating with each other."[132]

It does not seem reasonable to believe that crime will be deterred by simply materializing harsher sentences. The white-collar offender may weigh the risk of punishment, but the street offender most probably does not. With no job, no opportunity, no close family ties, he may well deduce that by committing a crime, or even by imprisonment, he has more to gain than to lose.

In conclusion, violence must be shown realistically, with all the negative consequences—with the hurt and long-range after-effects related to it. With real violence there is an aftermath of pain to the body and spirit; with television violence, on the other hand, the impact is over soon after the violent scene. Viewers must be aware of their intake and be capable of distinguishing what is entertainment for the sake of novelty, and what is *real* for the sake of mankind.

What immature, insecure people see others do, they will copy. It is interesting to note, for example, that before 1871 wife-beating was a husband's privilege in this country,[133] and that presently polls show that at least twenty-five percent of American men feel that they have the right to beat their wives.[134] Add this to the fact that twenty-five million American women are beaten by their husbands, and needless to say, a clear picture becomes evident.[135]

It is self-defeating to see ourselves as helpless, aggressive beings who will simply have to accept our innate meanness. Certainly there are certain dispositions toward intolerance and aggression in us, but "we carry no mark of Cain upon our brows. The thesis of man's killer nature cannot seriously be upheld; on the contrary, investigation shows that by nature we are also extremely friendly beings."[136]

In a recent NBC-TV news program about juvenile crime, John Chancellor interviewed several teenaged murderers. One, about to be released from a New York City juvenile detention center, casually admitted to fifteen murders, most of which occurred during muggings. Mr. Chancellor asked the boy, "What did you feel during and after the killings?"

"Nothing," he replied.

"Nothing? Even when they lay on the ground bleeding and gasping?" asked Mr. Chancellor.

"No, nothing. Nothing really! It was like watching a television play or a movie. It wasn't real."[137]

Notes

1. Jeffrey H. Goldstein, *Aggression and Crimes of Violence* (New York: Oxford University Press, 1975), p. x.
2. *Ibid.*, p. xi.
3. Sigmund Freud, *Civilization and Its Discontents* (New York: W. W. Norton Co., 1962).
4. Anthony Storr, *Human Aggression* (New York: Atheneum, 1968).
5. Nikolaas Tinbergen, "Behaviorist Thinks Aggression Is Both Instinctive & Learned," *The New York Times*, October 28, 1968, p. 6.
6. Gordon W. Allport, *The Nature of Prejudice* (Garden City, New York: Doubleday, Anchor Books, 1958, pp. 335-44, 460-61.
7. Fredric Wertham, *A Sign for Cain* (New York: Macmillan Co., 1966).
8. Ashley Montague, *Man and Aggression* (London: Oxford University Press, 1968).
9. Konrad Lorenz, *On Aggression* (New York: Bantam Books, 1967).
10. James G. Fraser, *The New Golden Bough* (Garden City, New York: Doubleday, 1959), pp. 289-315.
11. J. Bronowski, *The Face of Violence* (Cleveland: World Publishing Co., 1968), pp. 1-18.
12. Goldstein, *Op. cit.*, p. 4.
13. *Ibid.*, p. 10.
14. *Ibid.*
15. *Ibid.*
16. Ernest Jones, *Sigmund Freud* (London: Hogarth Press, 1955), Vol. II, p. 151.
17. Sigmund Freud, *New Introductory Lectures on Psycho-Analysis* (London: Hogarth Press & Institute of Psycho-Analysis, 1937), p. 139.
18. Sigmund Freud, *Beyond the Pleasure Principle* (London: London Press & Institute of Psycho-Analysis, 1948), p. 1.
19. Storr, *Op. cit.*, p. 8.

20. *Ibid.*, p. 11.
21. W. B. Cannon, *Bodily Changes in Pain, Hunger, Fear and Rage* (New York: Appleton, 1929).
22. Edwin Newman, "Violence in America," Channel 4 (NBC) Televised Special, January 5, 1977, 9-11 P.M. EST.
23. Saul Kapel, "Children Must Learn to Curb Aggression," *Daily News*, November 23, 1976, p. 40.
24. *Ibid.*
25. *Ibid.*
26. *Ibid.*
27. *Ibid.*
28. Seymour Feshbach, "The Young Aggressors," *Psychology Today*, April, 1973, p. 90.
29. *Ibid.*, p. 91.
30. *Ibid.*, p. 93.
31. Storr, *Op. cit.*, p. 15.
32. Feshbach, *Op. cit.*, p. 93.
33. *Ibid.*, p. 94.
34. Newman, *Op. cit.*
35. *Ibid.*
36. Elliot Aronson, "The Rationalizing Animal," *Psychology Today*, May, 1973, p. 46.
37. Sidney Siegal, *Choice, Strategy and Utility* (New York: McGraw-Hill Book Co., 1964), p. 3.
38. *Ibid.*, p. 8.
39. Robert P. Abelson, *Theories of Cognitive Consistency: A Sourcebook* (Chicago: Rand McNally & Co., 1968), p. 22.
40. *Ibid.*, p. 201.
41. *Ibid.*, p. 202.
42. *Ibid.*, p. 247.
43. *Ibid.*
44. *Ibid.*
45. *Ibid.*, p. 367.
46. *Ibid.*
47. *Ibid.*, p. 368.
48. *Ibid.*
49. *Ibid.*, p. 386.
50. Newman, *Op. cit.*
51. *Ibid.*
52. *Ibid.*
53. *Ibid.*
54. *Ibid.*
55. *Ibid.*
56. *Ibid.*
57. *Ibid.*

58. *Ibid.*
59. Goldstein, *Op. cit.*, p. 12.
60. Nikolaas Tinbergen, *The Study of Instinct* (Oxford: Clarendon, 1951).
61. Goldstein, *Op. cit.*, p. x.
62. *Ibid.*
63. *Ibid.*, p. 19.
64. *Ibid.*
65. *Ibid.*
66. E. Staub, "The Learning and Unlearning of Aggression: The Role of Anxiety, Empathy, Efficacy, and Prosocial Values." In J. L. Singer, ed., *The Control of Aggression and Violence*, pp. 93-124.
67. Goldstein, *Op. cit.*, pp. 23-24.
68. Seymour Feshbach, "Aggression." In P. H. Mussen, ed., *Carmichael's Manual of Child Psychology*. Vol. II (New York: Wiley, 1970), p. 173.
69. I. P. Pavlov, *Conditioned Reflexes* (New York: Oxford University Press, 1927).
70. C. A. Loew, "Acquisition of a Hostile Attitude and Its Relation to Aggressive Behavior," *Journal of Personality and Social Psychology*, 1967, 5, pp. 552-58.
71. M. R. Yarrow, J. D. Campbell and R. V. Burton, *Child Rearing: An Inquiry into Research and Methods* (San Francisco: Jossey-Bass, 1968).
72. R. R. Sears, E. E. Maccoby and H. Levin, *Patterns of Child Rearing* (Evanston, Illinois: Row & Peterson, 1957), p. 29.
73. *Ibid.*
74. Goldstein, *Op. cit.*, p. 29.
75. A. Bandura, *Aggression: A Social Learning Analysis* (Englewood Cliffs, New Jersey: Prentice-Hall, 1973).
76. A. Bandura, D. Ross and S. A. Ross, "Vicarious Reinforcement and Imitative Learning," *Journal of Abnormal and Social Psychology*, 1963, 67, pp. 601-7.
77. W. McCord, J. McCord and L. K. Zola, *Origins of Crime: A New Evaluation of the Cambridge-Somerville Youth Study* (New York: Columbia University Press, 1959).
78. Feshbach, *Op. cit.*, p. 94.
79. *Ibid.*, p. 95.
80. Goldstein, *Op. cit.*, p. 34.
81. *Ibid.*, pp. 34-36.
82. *Ibid.*, p. 37.
83. L. Berkowitz, "Some Aspects of Observed Aggression," *Journal of Personality & Social Psychology*, 1965, 2, pp. 359-69.
84. B. H. Kniveton, "The Effect of Rehearsal Delay on Long-Term

Imitation of Filmed Aggression," *British Journal of Psychology,*
1973, 64, pp. 259-65.

85. W. Mischel, *Introduction to Personality* (New York: Holt, Rinehart & Winston, 1971), p. 380.

86. R. J. Barndt and D. M. Johnson, "Time Orientation in Delinquents," *Journal of Abnormal & Social Psychology,* 1955, 51,
pp. 343-45.

87. A. Bandura & W. Mischel, "Modification of Self-Imposed Delay
of Reward Through Exposure to Live and Symbolic Models,"
Journal of Personality & Social Psychology, 1965, 2, pp. 698-
705.

88. W. Mischel and E. Staub, "Effects of Expectancy on Working &
Waiting for Larger Rewards," *Journal of Personality & Social
Psychology,* 1965, 2, pp. 625-33.

89. J. H. Crook, *The Nature and Function of Territorial Aggression* (New York: Oxford University Press, 1968), pp. 173-74.

90. Storr, *Op. cit.,* pp. 132-33.

91. Aronson, *Op. cit.,* p. 50.

92. *Ibid.*

93. *Ibid.*

94. W. Goode, "Violence Among Inmates" (Washington, D.C.:
U.S. Government Printing Office, 1969), p. 950.

95. Goldstein, *Op. cit.,* p. 61.

96. *Ibid.,* p. 69.

97. *Ibid.,* p. 70.

98. Lester Smith, "Crime Under Sixteen," Channel 9 (WOR)
Televised Special, April 13, 1977, 10-11 P.M. EST.

99. *Ibid.*

100. *Ibid.*

101. *Ibid.*

102. *Ibid.*

103. Fritz Redl and David Wineman, *The Aggressive Child* (Illinois:
The Free Press, 1957), p. 21.

104. *Ibid.,* p. 22.

105. *Ibid.,* pp. 29-30.

106. *Ibid.,* pp. 50-51.

107. *Ibid.,* pp. 120-21.

108. *Ibid.,* p. 143.

109. *Ibid.,* pp. 147-54.

110. *Ibid.,* pp. 156-65.

111. *Ibid.,* pp. 166-74.

112. *Ibid.,* pp. 175-93.

113. *Ibid.,* p. 290.

114. *Ibid.,* p. 291.

115. *Ibid.*, pp. 293-94.
116. *Ibid.*, pp. 296-97.
117. *Ibid.*, p. 303.
118. *Ibid.*, p. 306.
119. *Ibid.*, p. 308.
120. *Ibid.*, p. 311.
121. *Ibid.*, p. 415.
122. *Ibid.*, pp. 431-32.
123. *Ibid.*, pp. 473-74.
124. Goldstein, *Op. cit.*, p. 135.
125. *Ibid.*, p. 136.
126. *Ibid.*, pp. 140-41.
127. *Ibid.*, p. 139.
128. Arnold Arnold, *Violence and Your Child* (Chicago: Henry Regnery Co., 1969), pp. 178-87.
129. Feshbach, *Op. cit.*, p. 95.
130. David L. Bazelon, "Street Crime and Correctional Potholes," *Federal Probation*, March 1977 (Bazelon is the Chief Judge of the U.S. Court of Appeals at Washington, D.C.), p. 4.
131. *Ibid.*, pp. 4-5.
132. *Ibid.*, p. 6.
133. Stanley Siegal, "Women Beating," Channel 7 (ABC) Talk Host Show: ("The Stanley Siegal Show"), November 11, 1977, 9-10 A.M. EST.
134. *Ibid.*
135. *Ibid.*
136. Irenaus Eibl-Eibesfeldt, *Love and Hate* (New York: Holt, Rinehart & Winston, 1972), pp. 245-46.
137. Bryan W. Key, *Media Sexploitation* (New York: New American Library, 1976), p. 137.

Selected Bibliography

BOOKS

Alland, Alexander, Jr. *The Human Imperative.* New York: Columbia University Press, 1972.

Arnold, Arnold. *Violence and Your Child.* Chicago: Henry Regnery Co., 1969.

Allport, Gordon W. *The Nature of Prejudice.* Garden City, New York, Doubleday, Anchor Books, 1958.

Abelson, Robert P. *Theories of Cognitive Consistency: A Sourcebook.* Chicago: Rand McNally & Co., 1968.

Bach, George R. *Aggressiveness.* Garden City, New York: Doubleday, 1974.

Barber, Carolyn. *Aggressive Behavior in Animals.* New York: Harper & Row, 1971.

Bandura, A. *Aggression: A Social Learning Analysis.* Englewood Cliffs, New Jersey: Prentice Hall, 1973.

Bronowski, Jacob. *The Face of Violence.* Cleveland: World Publishing Co., 1968.

Cannon, W. B. *Bodily Changes in Pain, Hunger, Fear and Rage.* New York: Appleton, 1929.

Claiborne, Robert. *Aggressiveness.* New York: W. W. Norton Co., 1974.

Crook, J. H. *The Nature and Function of Territorial Aggression.* New York: Oxford University Press, 1968.

Demaris, Ovid. *America the Violent.* New York: Cowles Book Co., 1970.

Eibl-Eibesfeldt, Irenaus. *Love and Hate.* New York: Holt, Rinehart & Winston, 1972.

Freud, Sigmund. *Beyond the Pleasure Principle.* London: Hogarth Press & Institute of Psycho-Analysis, 1937.

Freud, Sigmund. *New Introductory Lectures on Psycho-Analysis.* London: Hogarth Press & Institute of Psycho-Analysis, 1937.

Freud, Sigmund. *Civilization and Its Discontents.* New York: W. W. Norton Co., 1962.

Fraser, James G. *The New Golden Bough.* Garden City, New York: Doubleday, 1959.

Goldstein, Jeffrey H. *Aggression and Crimes of Violence.* New York: Oxford University Press, 1975.

Goode, W. *Violence among Inmates.* Washington, D.C.: U.S. Government Printing Office, 1969.

Gray, Glenn *On Understanding Violence Philosophically.* New York: Harper & Row, 1970.

Gunn, John. *Violence.* New York: Praeger Publishers, 1973.

Jones, Ernest. *Sigmund Freud.* London: Hogarth Press, 1955.

Key, Bryan W. *Media Sexploitation.* New York: New American Library, 1976.

Liston, Robert A. *Violence in America.* New York: Julian Messner, 1976.

Lorenz, Konrad. *On Aggression.* New York: Bantam Books, 1967.

May, Rollo. *Aggressiveness.* New York: W. W. Norton Co., 1972.

McCord, W. *Origins of Crime.* New York: Columbia University Press, 1959

Mischel, W. *Introduction to Personality.* New York: Holt, Rinehart & Winston, 1971.

Montague, Ashley. *Man and Aggression.* New York: Oxford University Press, 1973.

Pavlov, I. P. *Conditioned Reflexes.* New York: Oxford University Press, 1927.

Redl, Fritz. *The Aggressive Child.* Illinois: The Free Press, 1957.

Sears, R. R. *Patterns of Child Rearing.* Evanston, Illinois: Row & Peterson, 1957.

Siegal, Sidney. *Choice, Strategy and Utility.* New York: McGraw-Hill Book Co., 1964.

Staub, E. *The Control of Aggression and Violence.* J. L. Singer, ed.

Storr, Anthony. *Human Aggression.* New York: Atheneum, 1968.

Tinbergen, Nikolaas. *The Study of Instinct.* Oxford: Clarendon, 1951.

Wertham, Frederic. *A Sign for Cain.* New York: Macmillan Co., 1966.

Yarrow, M. R. *Child Rearing: An Introduction into Research and and Methods.* San Francisco: Jossey-Bass, 1968.

JOURNALS AND MAGAZINES

Aronson, Elliot. "The Rationalizing Animal," *Psychology Today,* May, 1973.

Barndt, R. J. "Time Orientation in Delinquents," *Journal of Abnormal & Social Psychology,* 1955, 51.

Bazelon, David L. "Street Crime and Correctional Potholes," *Federal Probation,* March, 1977.

Berkowitz, Leon. "Some Aspects of Observed Aggression," *Journal of Personality & Social Psychology,* 1965, 2.

Feshbach, Norma and Seymour. "The Young Aggressors," *Psychology Today,* April, 1973.

Feshbach, Seymour. "Aggression," *Carmichael's Manual of Child Psychology,* Vol. II, New York: Wiley, 1970.

Klein, Helen A. *Federal Probation,* June, 1977.

Kniveton, B. H. *British Journal of Psychology,* 1973, 64.

Loew, C. A. "Acquisition of a Hostile Attitude and Its Relation to Aggressive Behavior," *Journal of Personality & Social Psychology,* 1965, 5.

NEWSPAPERS

Daily News, November 23, 1976.

The *New York Times,* October 28, 1968.

TELEVISION PROGRAMS

Newman, Edwin (Narrator). "Violence in America," Channel 4
    (NBC) January 5, 1977, 9-11 P.M. EST.
Siegal, Stanley (T.V. Talk Host). "Women Beating," Channel 7
    (ABC) November 11, 1977, 9-10 A.M. EST.
Smith, Lester (Narrator). "Crime Under Sixteen," Channel 9
    (WOR) April 13, 1977, 10-11 P.M. EST.